GERMAN SCHOOLBOY, BRITISH COMMANDO

GERMAN SCHOOLBOY, BRITISH COMMANDO

CHURCHILL'S SECRET SOLDIER

HELEN FRY

First published 2010

The History Press
The Mill, Brimscombe Port
Stroud, Gloucestershire, GL5 2QG
www.thehistorypress.co.uk

British Library Cataloguing in Publication Data.
A catalogue record for this book is available from the British Library.

ISBN 978 0 7524 4996 8

Typesetting and origination by The History Press
Printed in India by Aegean Offset Printers, New Delhi

To the Memory of Curt Ascher,
Colin Anson's father

who spoke out against Nazism in Germany,
for which he paid with his life
in Dachau concentration camp
on 15 October 1937

'One man asks what's the consequence? the other what is right?
And therein lies the difference between serf and knight.'

This was the principle by which Curt Ascher lived and by
which he died.

Contents

Acknowledgements   9

Introduction   11

Chapter   1   Early Years in Germany   13

Chapter   2   The Hitler Years   27

Chapter   3   Emigration   45

Chapter   4   The Pioneer Corps   57

Chapter   5   Commando Training   73

Chapter   6   The Invasion of Sicily   91

Chapter   7   Commando Raids   111

Chapter   8   The Liberation of Corfu   131

Chapter   9   Return to Frankfurt   147

Chapter 10   Civilian Life   159

Chapter 11   Postscript   169

Appendix 1   3 Troop detachment to No.2 Commando Brigade   171

Appendix 2   3 Troop detachment Commando training
                  schedules, Italy, 1945   173

Notes   179

Selected Bibliography   181

Index   183

Acknowledgements

I would like to express my heartfelt thanks to Colin Anson for sharing his extraordinary life story with me and enabling me to write this book. It has been a privilege for me as a historian to record his oral testimony and work on the life of a man with great dignity and moral principles whose bravery in the war deserves this complete recognition. Neither could this book have been written without the unswerving support and commitment of his wife Alice. She has been truly marvellous to both of us morally and supporting us with sustenance during our long interviews. Alice was also forced to flee from the Nazis; she was born in Vienna and subsequently also served in the British forces in the Second World War. I have grown exceptionally close to Colin and Alice and deem it a huge honour that he has entrusted me with some of his most personal and painful memories. He has had to re-live so much which he would rather have lay buried, but I managed to persuade him that his story deserves recording for posterity.

A special mention is due to Sophie Bradshaw, an exceptional Commissioning Editor, whose insight and vision have enabled stories to be published which may otherwise not have seen the light of day. That is true also for the immense dedicated support I have received over the few years from Peter Teale. He has supported my ideas and brought some of them to fruition. It is fun and stress-free working with him. Thanks to CEO Stuart Biles for his encouragement, also Simon Hamlet and the editorial team at The History Press for producing such a quality publication and with whom it is a real pleasure to work. I also wish to acknowledge the idiosyncratic Paul Savident whose support of my writing projects in so many diverse ways is much appreciated. My thanks also go to John Courtney of the British Local History website for his support of my writing career and promoting my research and books. I am exceptionally grateful to Alexia Dobinson for typing up the hours of interviews which I carried out for this book. She has been a real tower of strength and support.

Thanks are due also to Suzanne Bardgett, Director of the Holocaust Office at the Imperial War Museum, for her friendship and continued support to me in this field of research. I would like to acknowledge Colonel John Starling and Norman Brown of the Royal Pioneer Corps Association for their interest and support of my books. Thanks to Dirk Riedel at the Dachau Concentration Camp Archives in Germany for providing information about Colin's father in Dachau.

German journalist Matthias Martin-Becker, based in Berlin, has taken an active interest in these veteran stories, including a number of interviews for radio and newspapers about Colin. He has portrayed the story with sensitivity and accuracy. I have been fortunate to have the support and encouragement of staff at The Association of Jewish Refugees, including Howard Spier, Hazel Beiny and Esther Rinkoff. Many thanks to them.

Mary Curry of Barnstaple, a special friend, is to be accredited with starting off a whole series of books which has led to this biography. She has read and commented on every draft of the chapters for this book, and for that I am immensely grateful and could not do without her critical eye and sharp mind.

I have an exceptional network of friends who continue to support my work. To them, I owe a huge debt of gratitude: to my loyal friend James Hamilton who has built up a remarkable creative and dynamic partnership with me on writing historical novels under the pseudonym of J.H. Schryer; also to Elkan Levy, Edith Palmer, Colin Hamilton, Jon Russell and Richard Bernstein.

This book could not have been written without the support of my family: my husband Martin, our sons Jonathan, David and Edward, and my mother Sandra. Thank you.

Introduction

Sitting in the armchair opposite me in a bungalow in Hertfordshire is a relaxed gentleman in his late eighties. His kind, gentle manner, and firm Prussian accent which carefully forms each English word he utters, hide a lifetime of bravery. He explains that he has done nothing extraordinary or brave during the Second World War. I soon discover that this is certainly not the case. He was not born in England; neither was his name originally Colin Anson. He was born in Germany as Claus Leopold Octavio Ascher. After his immigration to England, Colin was one of the 10,000 German refugees from Nazism who served in the British armed forces during the Second World War.

During the many hours that I spent interviewing him, I soon learnt that this tender giant had the most intensive physical training the British Army could offer. He learnt to undertake missions which would make most people shudder. And yet it is still possible to tell by looking at him, even sixty-five years later, that the toned figure of this eighty-eight-year-old veteran has been through elite commando training. In the summer of 1943 he was involved in the invasion of Sicily with the Royal Marine Commandos, was severely wounded in action, died on the operating table and was revived after half an hour. He recovered and nine months later was determined to re-join his unit, which he did. He was then involved in commando raids behind enemy lines and in front-line combat. He was based on the Yugoslav island of Vis from where he and his comrades carried out attacks on other islands. It was not just the enemy who were to be feared; the commandos could never be quite sure whether local partisans would treat them as allies or betray them. Colin took part in the invasion of Albania and finally the liberation of Corfu.

What emerges very early on in my interviews with Colin is his strong ethical grounding which permeates the most life-defining decisions. That came from two major influences in his life: his father and his upbringing with his Protestant Youth Group. Even decades later, it is possible to see how Colin was deeply affected and shaped, for the better, by his father's strong sense of right and wrong. That man's determination to stand up to the Nazi regime and the consequences he suffered as a result, have left a deep and lasting impression on Colin. At the end of the war, and stationed back in Frankfurt, this one-time German schoolboy turned British commando stood at the crossroads of a moral dilemma. Should he exact revenge on the lock-keeper who had betrayed his father to the Gestapo?

When it came to recording Colin's post-war civilian life, I asked him about his hobbies. I should have guessed – what does an ex-commando with plenty of charisma and panache do? In characteristic vein, he takes up flying and becomes a glider pilot!

Colin, with his comrades, was amongst those who fought a real war, a tough and dangerous war; one which had seen him severely injured and dying in the field of action. Today he sees nothing extraordinary in having sacrificed his life and freedom for King and adopted Country. For him, this had been his war. It was his duty to do what he could to defeat Hitler and Nazism.

German Schoolboy, British Commando is his extraordinary story.

CHAPTER 1

Early Years in Germany

My dear sir, if a year ago you had ventured to predict that your lady wife would this day be delivered of a healthy boy, I would have said to you: 'my dear sir, you are a great optimist'.

These words were uttered by Berlin doctor Dr Bökelmann to Curt Ascher on the birth of his son, Claus Leopold Octavio Ascher. It was 13 February 1922; the address Dr Bökelmann's clinic at 13 Augsburger Strasse in the Charlottenburg district of Berlin. At the time the Aschers were living at Apostel Paulus Str. 13, Berlin-Schöneberg. The birth was miraculous because the previous year Curt's wife, Mathilde, had suffered from a gynaecological condition which meant child-bearing seemed nigh on impossible. On 11 June 1922 this healthy boy was baptised in the Dreifaltigkeits Kirche by Pastor Lahusen, a distant relative of Mathilde Ascher. As one-time head of the Evangelical Church in Germany, Pastor Lahusen had been dubbed 'The Protestant Pope'.

Claus Ascher was raised a Protestant. His mother was Protestant, his father Jewish. His father's Jewish roots did not pose a problem until the 1930s when Hitler came to power in Germany. His earliest memory was as a toddler in Berlin, seated on the carpet in the dining room, when his mother entered the room with a shopping net containing a yellow wooden racing car. It became his most treasured toy. His childhood was a secure, happy existence, nurtured by loving parents in comfortable surroundings. His father saw himself first and foremost as German, his Jewish background secondary. Curt Ascher was born on 12 December 1882 in Glatz, then a small Prussian county town in Upper Silesia, now Klodzko in Poland. It was there that he grew up as the only son in a family of seven. Three sisters were older than him, three younger.

> My father was therefore rather spoilt. Educated at a boarding school, he enjoyed fast horses. In due course he had a scar from the top of his head to his forehead from a time when he drove too fast on a main road with a dogcart (a two-wheeled horse drawn carriage). Motor-cars were very much in their infancy at the end of the 1890s into the early 1900s and so my father enjoyed driving a dogcart. One day he went too fast and an accident occurred on one of the rough mountain roads in the Riesengebirge (Giant Mountains) near Glatz. One of the wheels hit a large stone, upsetting the cart. He needed stitches to his forehead and whilst his wound was being stitched, it kept bursting open. He was rather proud of his sang-froid in asking the doctor whether he could sew on some buttons, so he could do it up himself! (Zippers had not yet been invented).

Curt Ascher owned a brewery and theatre in Glatz. He had first studied chemistry at Breslau and belonged to a Jewish students' duelling fraternity at the university there. The Jewish members tended to attract a disproportionate number of challenges such that Curt fought a number of duels, but he despised the pride of those German students with duelling scars which, he felt, merely showed them up as bad fencers.

Curt eventually took over the brewery in Glatz. However, his business affairs were always rather up and down, though this was not always his fault. The larger brewers began to undercut the smaller ones, putting them out of business. Things began to go wrong for Curt. He had by now married Käte Seidel from Breslau. They had a daughter, Claus's half-sister Suzanne, born in 1910 and twelve years older than him. Business life became tough, causing much tension in Curt's relationship with his in-laws. They did not want to bail him out financially and things were about to get worse for him. One day, on a rather hot evening, he was at a party. The windows were open and as the local voluntary fire brigade clanged past, he leant out of the window to ask a member of the crew he knew, 'where's the fire?' The reply came, 'in the brew house'. This was, of course, his own business premises. In accordance with ancient regulations, the wooden buildings beneath the stone fortress of Glatz could not be insured. The old ordinance forbade the erection of buildings in the glacis of the fortress which could not be quickly demolished to clear a field of fire. The buildings which complied with that regulation were wooden and therefore uninsurable. Both the brewery and theatre were destroyed. With no insurance protection, Curt's loss was total and his business collapsed. Now his already fraught relationship with his wife and her family were severely strained.

Curt and Käte divorced in about 1912. Curt found a position with the Foreign Office in Berlin and moved to the city. In due course he was to have been sent to Turkey as commercial attaché at the German Embassy, but the face of Europe was changing. The First World War of 1914–18 intervened and he was to serve in the German army instead. Under universal conscription, he had been called up when of military age like all male Germans. The normal duration of service was two years, but the sons of families who could afford it could pay for an abbreviated service with certain privileges. Curt served as '*Einjährig-Freiwilliger*' (one year volunteer) with his regiment and was then, like everyone else, in the reserves.

At the outbreak of war in the summer of 1914, Curt was required to serve with his regiment. The heir apparent to the Austro-Hungarian Empire, Archduke Franz Ferdinand, and his wife Princess Sophie had been assassinated on 28 June as their carriage drove through the streets of Sarajevo in Bosnia.[1] The assassination, perpetrated by the Bosnian-born fanatic Princip, precipitated the outbreak of war. Germany's neighbour, Austria, declared war on Serbia. Troops now began to mobilise across Europe, with Russia amassing forces at the border. Russia backed Serbia against Austria-Hungary; Germany supported Austria against Russia; France supported Russia against Germany which precipitated Germany's pre-emptive action against France (Schlieffen Plan) bringing Britain into the war as well.[2] Great Britain declared war on Germany on 4 August 1914 after German troops invaded Belgium. In the ensuing year, 1914–15, German successes made victory over Britain, France and Russia seem likely.

There was every hope on both sides of the English Channel that the war would not last long. Having been called up, Curt Ascher was proud to fight for Germany and was conscripted into a signals branch of the infantry, serving with his regiment in France. In 1916 he fought in the trenches at the Battle of the Somme. The battle lasted several months from July 1916 to the winter of 1916. Morale on both sides was low. Many young lives were lost and the misery of the mud and the bloody massacres became lasting images of the First World War. The scenes of horror, death and the horrendous injuries sustained by many soldiers depressed both sides:

My father did not talk much about the war. It was such a terrible experience for him. From the little he did tell me, it was whilst in France with his unit that he had to creep out of the trenches at night sometimes to fit induction coils round the French field telephone wires to intercept their communications.

The raging battles on the front line meant that men had a slim chance of survival or escape from injury and at the Somme Curt Ascher was badly wounded. He was buried when shell fire caused his trench to cave in and he had to be dug out. He sustained a potentially life-threatening injury when shell splinters penetrated his skull. They remained there for the rest of his life: 'this was ironic because in the next war, the Second World War,' comments his son, 'I would sustain the same injury to the skull but on the other side to him.' Curt Ascher was in a coma for about a week and when he recovered was no longer fit for front-line fighting.

After a period of recovery he was posted to the city of Cologne in charge of anti-aircraft searchlights. His command post, in a pillar of the old Cologne suspension bridge over the Rhine, has since been demolished. He used the searchlights to illuminate the cathedral of Cologne, something he would never have dreamt of doing in the Second World War. The range of British aircraft extended that far in the First World War but their priorities were military targets rather than cities. Based in Cologne, Curt could serve out the rest of the war in relative security. Life was pleasant until one day he said to his orderly at breakfast:

> 'There's no butter.'
> And the orderly said, 'No sir.'
> 'Well, go out and buy some.'
> 'I've tried that sir, and there is none to be bought.'

It was at that moment that he realised the war was lost. It was now early November 1918. Just a few days later on 11 November, at the eleventh hour of the eleventh day of the eleventh month, Germany signed an armistice. Europe was reeling at the human cost of four years of bloody fighting. Millions of young men lay dead, many with graves as unknown soldiers. It was hoped that Europe would never again witness such carnage. Soon everything disintegrated into chaos. For Germany it was a bitter peace, the consequences of which would be played out in the 1930s with devastating results. Claus comments:

> There had been no psychological or other contingency plan for such an eventuality. Germany was not psychologically prepared for defeat. The Kaiser abdicated and went off to his estates in Holland. Some military units returned; others just disintegrated.

With the peace signed, Curt Ascher returned home to Berlin. He headed the political department of the *Reichswehr*, as an official in the defence ministry, the *Reichswehrministerium*. He served under the first ever Social Democratic Defence

Minister Gustav Noske. 'My father respected him enormously,' says Claus. 'Noske was a man of resolution and great courage. It was he who gave me the pistol still hanging on my wall, a ladies' flintlock pistol made by Adams of London, and was then 250 years old.' Noske was a Social Democrat and union man, one of the few politicians that people would heed after the First World War. He was one of those who had the courage to try to put Germany back on a positive and constructive basis. As a young boy, Claus heard tales from Noske of his success which led to his appointment as Minister of Defence:

> He was *one* of the brave and principled people who had the courage of grasping the nettle to try to bring order out of the chaos. When the navy rebelled, it was based at Kiel and there was a critical meeting of the German Navy there. It was Noske who was sent to Kiel to talk them round and settle the dispute. Noske told me how he was rowed out in a boat to the big battleship which was the headquarters of the mutineers. They let down a series of ladders for him to climb up the side to board the ship, the height of a house. He was about half way up when he wondered how much further they would let him climb before they tipped the ladder over. But he did get to the top, the mutineers helped him over the railings and after forty-eight hours of non-stop talking, he managed to get them to adopt a positive point of view and co-operate. It was on the basis of his success that he was appointed the first defence minister of Germany after the war.

Post-war Europe was being shaped by the Allied powers. Germany could only bow to their demands. Under the conditions of the Treaty of Versailles, drawn up in the summer of 1919, Germany was forbidden to amass military forces, the quota restricted to a maximum of 100,000 men without armoured vehicles, heavy weapons or an air force. Curt Ascher's work in the *Reichswehr* became necessary in these new turbulent times when the corrosive influence of the complete collapse of German politics and morals had set in. The German people looked at the Russian collapse after the 1917 Revolution and its declaration as a Socialist Soviet Republic. There was a real danger that political unrest and instability in Germany could lead the same way, but only some sections of the German people wanted to go that far. It fell to the *Reichswehr* to keep some kind of order in post-war Germany so that a new start could be made.

There were military units like the Freikorps who were under the command of right-wing officers and they wanted to reinstate what had been before, namely a militarist Prussian monarchy. It was sometimes better to co-operate with them, thereby exercising influence, rather than letting them roam like loose cannon. Bavaria seceded from the Reich and formed an independent Soviet Socialist

Republic. The violent role played by the Freikorps in quelling that secession was a distasteful and regrettable necessity, but Bavaria was brought back into the new German Republic. Immediately after the war, the *Reichswehr* had to deal with the military disturbance of the 1918–19 Spartacus Rebellion.

On one occasion at this time Curt Ascher's driver may have saved his life. Everyday Curt was driven to the *Reichswehrministerium*. As they approached the building one day, they saw a crowd of Spartacists, armed and trying to fire at them. Curt's driver put his foot right down, drove straight at them. The crowd opened up and he was able to get around the corner without being shot. On another occasion on the way to work, Curt's driver suddenly swerved into the middle of the road and went through the central arch of the Brandenburg Gate:

> My father was completely taken aback because until recently this was reserved for the Kaiser and no one else. My father exclaimed 'what on earth are you doing?' The reply came back: 'Many happy returns, sir. Happy Birthday'.

The *Reichswehr* was under the direct command of von Seeckt, a Prussian General, who was considered a very honourable man. It was his genuine aim to shape the new *Reichswehr* into a non-political servant of the new republic. He successfully managed to suppress the Spartacus Rebellion, but it remained a very turbulent time in Germany.

It was against this political backdrop that Curt Ascher made his own contribution to the new Germany. His work included fostering good relations within the army itself. Meanwhile, Gustav Noske as the new defence minister hoped to raise a genuine people's army, as Colin (then Claus) explains:

> Noske was a Social Democrat but in those days the kind of people he would have wanted, were the last people who would join the army and parade up and down. In the last few weeks of the First World War, there were still patriotic speeches and articles in the newspapers about German victory, but when the final collapse came, Germans were totally and psychologically unprepared. That was why there was such a back lash and revulsion in Germany against everything that had gone before, i.e. against the ruling class, the administrative class, and above all against the military classes. That is why my father's work was very important at this time.

As a government official and a former senior NCO, Curt became involved in the Association for the Protection of Upper Silesia, the county of his birth, at a time when the Poles wanted to annex the area. Curt was based in Berlin but began to travel abroad, to countries like Sweden, to learn about Swedish sport and physical training ideas. It was he who introduced sport into the German army. He recognised that competitive sport could act as a unifying force by giving the soldiers something positive to focus on during the turbulent times. In that sense, he had great insight. This was extended and he instituted *Volkshochschulen* (people's high schools) into the army whereby colleges were set up within the army. It enabled soldiers to pursue further studies in various subjects. It gave them a sense of achievement and qualifications; something positive to work for. Curt's central motivation was his realisation that the army needed a positive frame of mind. It was a fulfilling position for Curt in which he had the opportunity to implement positive ideas.

But Curt's job at the *Reichswehr* came to an abrupt end when a right-wing journalist and politician, von Kapp, wanted to lead a right-wing government and staged a putsch (a *coup d'état*). The military commander of the putsch was von Lüttwitz. He and his officers were well prepared. The group arrived in Berlin in a fleet of taxis with their secretaries and typewriters, ready to take over the seat of government. They moved into government premises and the government itself retreated to Dresden. The officers were in charge for a while, but had not planned ahead for what they would do once they had succeeded in power. The German people became impatient and a number of strikes broke out. The 'new' government did not know what to do next. After five days they packed up, took off in a fleet of taxis and that was the end of the putsch.

Noske received the brunt of the blame for the putsch and resigned. Curt Ascher followed suit and handed in his resignation. Noske became governor of the state of Hanover, a position which he held until deposed by the Nazis. It was then that he moved to the south of Frankfurt. Noske and Curt remained good friends and Noske would visit the Ascher house when they too were living in Frankfurt.

In 1920 Curt remarried in Berlin to Mathilde Ruyter (born 1882), originally from Bremen and a distant relative of the Dutch Admiral de Ruyter, the Grand Admiral of Holland.[3] Two years later, on 13 February 1922, their only child, a son Claus, was born. Before Claus's birth, Mathilde had been a professional opera singer. She particularly liked Verdi and musical ensembles and built up her career by going from one opera house to another, all over Germany. Every state capital in Germany had its playhouse and opera house. It was possible for Mathilde to further her career by going from one to the other, and each time always a step up. She was at Barsinghausen as the understudy of the lead role, but the star fell ill:

My mother had to jump in at a moment's notice. She knew the opera because she had been singing in a supporting role, but it took a few days and nights of strong coffee and little sleep to study the lead role properly. She was a huge success and was thereafter known as 'Our Aida'. Eventually from there she went to the Volks Opera in Hamburg where she sang as principal soprano. By now it was 1910 and Mathilde was at the peak of her career. At the Stadttheater she was leading soprano. Then she had an offer to audition at Dresden, the most renowned opera house in Germany at the time and an operatic Mecca with the standing of opera houses like Milan, Covent Garden and the Metropolitan of New York. It was an opportunity not to be missed. Unfortunately she contracted a throat infection, but dosed herself, determined still to sing. Sing she did but she ruined her voice and was forbidden to do so again for a year. That break had consequences for her career. After being out for so long, it was extremely difficult to resume a singing career and then the 1914–18 war intervened. She became a typist in the Ministry of Food. It was the love of music that brought her and my father together. My father possessed great musical appreciation and joined a choir in Berlin, for fun and relaxation as much as anything else. It was the same choir to which my mother belonged. They married in the same year of the Kapp Putsch.

After the wedding in 1920 Curt became Director of the *Industrie Film Aktiengesellschaft* (AG), a period marked by reasonable success. He had already been on the board as government representative and then became managing director after his resignation following the Kapp Putsch.

Curt travelled to Argentina to drum up business with important exports and cattle trade. He was absent for many months and, unfortunately by the time he came back, he found that the other director had ruined the company and embezzled money from it. Curt was not going to be associated with 'unclean business', so he declared the company bankrupt and started a lawsuit against him. The case dragged on for twelve years. Curt set up a private enterprise on his own as a public relations and advertising consultant. It was then that he moved with his wife and son Claus to the spa town of Bad Homburg:

I remember the day we moved from Berlin. I was still quite young, about four years old. I was sitting astride a suitcase playing motorbikes. The sun was streaming through the window but the room was bare. It used to be my father's office but now his desk had gone, so too the carpets. All that remained was the telephone on the window sill. We moved to a house in Bad Homburg and occupied the ground floor and basement. My father worked from home and travelled a lot. In his new business he contracted foreign firms like Brown-Boveri, a machine tool company in Switzerland, and I.T. Ronnefeld who were tea importers. He was able to build up a reasonable living and we had a comfortable life in Bad Homburg. My mother did not work; her role was always as housewife and mother. We had a cook and also a nursemaid for me called Anna von Brenneke whom I nicknamed Nacke, of whom I was very fond. We did not have a motor car – that was for rich people. It was in Bad Homburg that I started my first school. Because my half-sister Suzanne lived with her mother, who had also remarried, I was mostly in adult company and therefore rather precocious. I jumped one year of primary school and only had three years there. Henceforth I was always the youngest in my class, bullied quite a bit, and never really caught up because I was rather lazy. That loss of one year at school didn't do me any favours. Suzanne visited us in the holidays, but in effect I grew up as an only child. Our house had a large garden with several sloping lawns. In winter we tried to ski down in the snow. We had an Alsatian dog called Lona. My father preferred going to church, not because he was religious but because he enjoyed organ music. He lived by the straight, honest, Protestant moral and work ethic of north German Protestantism. We didn't normally go to church, but my mother used to sing the alto solo parts (her voice became lower in later life) in Christmas and Easter Oratorios in Church. Later when we lived at Frankfurt I used to go to confirmation classes and was duly confirmed at the age of thirteen. I did not even know that my father was Jewish until the Nazis came. It was then, and only then, that my father made a point of informing me that he was Jewish.

Claus has strong memories of the gorgeous summers spent in Bad Homburg, a place which hosted many cultural activities and flower shows. Its pleasant climate is protected by the Taunus mountains, a town with a promenade and health springs where people came to take cure:

There were young ladies at the wells in apron and cap serving foul-tasting spa water which you take for your liver or spleen. At the end of the promenade, a shell-shape bandstand in which there was the Kur Orchester. It performed all through the season under the baton of Herr Holger who then eloped with singer Ria Ginster which caused quite a scandal at the time. The first violin of the Kur Orchester was Gustav Lenzewski. He became a very good friend of the family, and later when we lived at Kaiser Friedrich Promenade, Gustav, on his way to the bandstand, would always call on us and have breakfast on the terrace. My mother had to behead the eggs for him because he could not risk cutting his finger.

Gustav Lenzewski later became a professor of music in Frankfurt, founded the Lenzewski Quartet and was an important exponent of modern music. He and his wife Ina became very good friends of Claus's mother when times turned difficult under the Nazis in 1937 and 1938. Guests were frequently at the Ascher house in those Bad Homburg days and it made for a very stimulating life. Claus recalls:

> We lived in a Victorian Gothic building with balconies surrounded by a large garden with lawns. By the top gate, there were woods where we walked our Alsatian dog Lona. The house was at Kuranlage 1. We went out picking mushrooms and my mother would then make the most beautiful mushroom soups. We had a thick textbook to check that we picked the right mushrooms and one on the different kinds of birds to learn about the peculiarities of the birds in our garden. We had a bird table on a window ledge. In the mornings we would suddenly see three claws appearing, and then the bird would pull itself up to look over and get busy on the fats and bread. The last to visit the table was a gorgeous woodpecker. Rather shy, it surveyed the scene from a nearby tree, then tucked in when the other birds had gone. It was a wonderful place to live.
>
> We got involved in the musical life in Bad Homburg. They were golden years. My parents retained their musical connections with Berlin and as such got to know musicians in the Berlin Philharmonic Orchestra. Later when we lived in Bad Homburg and they were on tour at Frankfurt, some of them would stay with us. This included double bass player Leberecht Goedeke and flautist Heinz Breiden.

One guest at Bad Homburg in the summer of 1930 was the British concert pianist Harriet Cohen.[4] She was invited to play at the International Music Festival in Bad Homburg with the Frankfurt Symphony Orchestra under Constant Lambert. During her visit she stayed at the Ritters Park Hotel, which at that time was the most prestigious hotel near the Concert Hall. She was engaged to perform William Walton's *Sinfonia Concertante* and Bax's *Symphony No.4*. While she was away, Harriet Cohen needed somewhere to practice piano for several hours a day. It was the Ascher family that offered their piano at their home at Kaiser Friedrich Promenade. Harriet Cohen left her mark on the eight-year-old Claus: 'My parents offered our Steinway Grand for Harriet Cohen to practice on. I remember that she was very beautiful and elegant and wore lovely drop earrings. I was very impressed by her.' As a souvenir of her visit, Harriet Cohen left the Aschers a signed postcard photograph of herself with Nobel Prize author George Bernard Shaw. On the reverse she wrote:

> To Mr & Mrs Ascher, with love from Harriet Cohen. Souvenir of the English Music Week at Bad Homburg, July 1930.

In 1932 Claus and his father visited Claus's half-sister Suzanne who was studying at Heidelberg University. During that trip, two soldiers caught Claus's attention: 'Soldiers are always a matter of interest to a ten-year-old boy,' he says, 'but especially for me it was exciting because Bad Homburg was in a demilitarised zone. I dug my father in the ribs and said: "Look, daddy, soldiers!" Whereupon he put on his stony face and said sharply "They are English – you do *not* look at them!" He was a very patriotic German, but in the light of what was to follow, I'm sure he would have approved when later I became a British soldier.'

Life was about to change for the Aschers. There was one particular dividing line in their lives. The lawsuit that Curt had begun against his business partner, which had dragged on for twelve years, finally came to a decision just before the Nazi period. Curt eventually won his legal battle against his partner at the same time as the partner was being sent to prison for another embezzlement. It was a mean justice and came at great cost to Curt. His business partner had no means to pay for the loss of business or legal costs. Although the partner was ordered to pay all the costs, he had not the means; a pyrrhic victory:

> My father had to pay his own legal fees. The cost of a twelve-year lawsuit was enormous. It cut things from under my father's feet. That, coupled with the rise of the Nazis to power in Germany the following year, ruined my father financially and marked *the* turning point in our fortunes. Our finances totally collapsed. The bailiffs came and took away the grand piano and other items. At that point, my mother took me to north Germany to visit her brother and other relations to ask for help. I wasn't aware of it at the time, because they didn't discuss finances with me.

In the summer of 1932, Claus was taken off to Vegesack, a small village along the river Weser, ten miles north-west of Bremen. It was by the Wümme and Lesum, tributaries of the river Weser, that the family had their country places, but Germany had been through a great deal of change and upheaval. Some family members fared well, but others had been ruined by the effects of the First World War and hyperinflation. Some of them still lived in large houses, others had moved into the gatekeeper's lodge. Claus and his mother stayed at a pension, a small guest house, at St Magnus on the river Lesum. During this time his father was trying to find his feet after the catastrophe, coping with being sued for debts and building up more business. Although these affairs were never discussed with the young Claus, it seems that his father also spent the time looking for new accommodation in Frankfurt now that their possessions and the apartment at Bad Homburg had gone. Claus and his mother went to stay near relatives until Curt sorted himself out. One solution, suggested by Mathilde, was that she should find work to help, but 'father had some old-fashioned attitudes, and when my mother suggested finding work, his pride exploded. He exclaimed that he'd rather shoot himself.' During this period Claus attended school in Vegesack. He recalls:

I spent much of that summer in the river swimming whilst my mother sat under a tree reading a book. It was here that my mother's cousin whom I always addressed as 'uncle' gave me his bicycle to learn to ride. Unfortunately he was 6ft tall and the saddle too high, so he removed it, wound sacking around the point of the triangle frame, and added wooden blocks to the pedals. Provided I could find somewhere to get onto the bicycle, I could stay on it. A local man helped me by pushing me along. He would grab hold of a strut of the bicycle frame and make sure that I didn't topple over. Learning how to ride a bicycle was in my mind always connected with the clip clop, clip clop of his wooden clogs running behind me, until the day came when he said, 'I wasn't holding it.' I had heard the clip, clop, clip clop which gave me confidence to ride but little did I know that it was unaided. It was on this enormous bicycle that I went to school, even in winter. Later, I got a season ticket and went by train. In that flat country, the snow would heap up in enormous drifts once it got on top of the dykes and dunes where the road was. If it was cold enough I could take a run up as hard as I could, and manage to go up and over. If the snow wasn't quite as hard packed as that or not frozen, I would go up and crash into it, then I had to drag the bicycle through the snow until the next milestone.

We visited our relatives from time to time and I remember one wonderful family birthday party when I was very impressed by the two sons of the 'birthday boy', both a little older than I. They met us at the gates to the estate in a motor car to drive us up to the house. Another large house, built of light-coloured stone, shimmered like a strange white wedding cake at night in the moonlight. It was there that my mother in her youth, while staying at a house party, had walked through a glass door without realising that it was closed. Fortunately she was not badly cut. The house was since demolished, and the grounds are now a public park.

Claus saw very little of his mother's brother Hans (Johann Ludwig Ruyter), his 'uncle Mori' or his wife Margaret. Aunt Margaret was a disagreeable woman who was not popular in the family. Claus was later told that when he was very young, they had visited Uncle Hans and Aunt Margaret. Claus had been put in Aunt Margaret's bed for a sleep but had wet the bed. His aunt was duly horrified and had exclaimed: 'Oh! My beautiful French bed!' to which Claus's nursemaid Nacke had tartly replied: 'Just as well it wasn't a German bed then!'

The political face of Germany was changing. A penniless painter and decorator was about to become the new chancellor. It was now 30 January 1933. It was in St Magnus that the ten-year-old Claus Ascher witnessed Adolf Hitler's rise to power.

CHAPTER 2

The Hitler Years

For the young Claus, the Nazi ascent to power appeared exciting. Men in smart uniforms, flags with swastikas, military songs, a new leader with great promises of restoring German pride, the offer of work for everyone, it all seemed like a unifying force for the good of the people. 'It was all very seductive,' he says. Germany was swept away on a wave of euphoria and the hope of a better world. Claus is clear about the motivations which brought Hitler to power:

Politics had always been rather visible in our household. The attitude had always been a moderate, responsible one, and opposed to ranting extremism. My father tended normally to vote for moderate right-of-centre parties or, in times of political turbulence, 'Centrum', the catholic centre party, for the sake of supporting stability. When once he saw a communist group march past he smiled approvingly, glad to see some opposition to the increasingly belligerent Nazi Stormtroopers, they gave him a clenched-fist salute. Which made him smile even more broadly, thinking of the salute they would have given him if they had been aware of the anti-communist role he had played when he was in the *Reichswehr Ministerium*.

I was not totally naïve even as an eleven year old boy but I too was caught up in the wave of fervour. The underlying resentment from the shame of losing the First World War, for which Germans were so psychologically and totally unprepared, was one of the main, if not *the* main, motivating forces which brought the Nazis to power. It was always smouldering under the surface.

Initially I could not see anything wrong. We were Germans first and foremost; Jewishness was not a topic of relevance in our household until Hitler came. Then one day my father told me that he was Jewish and pressed upon me to have a closer look at what was happening. His emphasis was not on his Jewish background threatening personal danger, but opposition to the aggressive and intolerant doctrinaire nationalistic fanaticism of a one-party police state being imposed. He declared his Jewish background out of principle, so as not to sail under a false flag.

The immediate difference of the regime was not personal for the Ascher family, although that would change. The 1920s had been a difficult decade for Germany who had been humiliated after the First World War and forced to pay huge reparations to Britain and France. Economically, Germany was on its knees, when Adolf Hitler roused the people with promises of work and the restoration of German pride. There was so much resentment at the 'lost war'. High inflation and mass unemployment in the post-war years cut from the feet of any successive German government that was trying to build the country up again. Claus reflects: 'Someone like Adolf Hitler with his sloganeering approach was something which began to restore national pride, confidence and self-respect.' Claus was in North Germany with his mother at the time. His father who was frequently away on business trips came to see them. His words to Claus during that visit left a lasting impression:

It was he who started to open my eyes. He was very politically aware and refused to deny what the Hitler regime really meant for Germany. He said to me, 'look under the surface. Look behind the stage set. See what this is leading to.' He was always against any extremist views of whatever persuasion.

The regime very quickly targeted Jewish intellectuals and their works. From 1933, Germany witnessed a 'brain-drain'. Jewish intellectuals, forbidden from holding public roles by the new regime, sought ways to immigrate to Britain, America or Palestine. German culture was disintegrating at an alarming rate, a formidable indicator of worse to come. On 10 May 1933, after less than four months in power, Joseph Goebbels, the Nazi Minister of Propaganda, ordered the burning of 'undesirable' books of leading Jewish intellectuals. That included the works of such Jewish intellectual giants as Karl Marx and Sigmund Freud. In Berlin's university square, academics and students gathered to begin an action that would see the burning of some 20,000 books. In ritualistic fashion, they hurled the books into the funeral pyre to the chant of:

Against soul-disintegrating exaggeration of the instinctive life for the nobility of the human soul, I commit to the flames the writings of ....

It was an act of monumental sacrilege, the betrayal of the freedom of thought. Such actions were incomprehensible to upright respectable Germans like Claus's father. He was deeply patriotic until the Nazis came to power. He loved the country of his birth, but now he was under no illusion of where Germany was heading and the consequences of the new regime. After about a year, he started to visit old army friends in Berlin in the hope of mobilising some kind of opposition to the Nazi government. He knew that the German industrialists were financing the stormtroopers, SS and private armies. They supported 'the Party' against the 'Red Peril' – the Russian revolutionary trend. Curt Ascher made no secret of his ideological views. This became an extremely dangerous position to hold and his business suffered. He hoped to persuade the Generals to do something to rein in the regime, but they wanted nothing to do with the establishment of any anti-Nazi Party. His views had a decided effect on his son back at home:

Meanwhile my father continued to urge me to look under the surface of the impressive military uniforms. Whilst he made me look twice at events in Germany, it was not possible to go back to how I was – a naïve school boy. I could no longer display an unquestioning enthusiasm for the regime. I had been made to think and could not return to innocence. The Nazis relieved people of the need to think for themselves. Responsibility had been handed over to the leaders. But for me, I had been made by my father to see through the façade and there was no turning back. It was suggested in the early days that my father should emigrate, but he brusquely denied that possibility. His view was 'I was born here, grew up here and fought for Germany in the war. I am German, I worked for the country and I will die here'.

Gustav Noske, Curt's friend and colleague who had been forced to resign as Governor of Hanover when the Nazis came to power, came to live with his wife at Frankfurt-Sachsenhausen. They were not far from the Aschers and the two families visited each others' homes. Noske did not shy away from his friendship with the Aschers, even though Curt was Jewish. On one particular outing together, there was a festive rally of the 'Schild' sports organisation in which he had been accepted as a member through a personal contact, although he was not Jewish. At this event, Claus and another member of the fencing section acted as colour guards in their fencing gear, complete with foils. His father attended with Noske, who came as a gesture of solidarity with this Jewish group. He recalls his father's action in protecting Noske:

We were drawn up in front of a tall fence at the edge of the field, unaware that behind it there was a turkey farm! When the turkeys all started gobbling in unison, it was very difficult to keep a straight face. What I clearly remember is a press photograph of the guests in which my father thrust himself into the picture deliberately to mask Noske to protect him from possible consequences of being photographed in the newspapers with a Jewish assembly. My father was conscious of the possible consequences for Noske of associating publicly with Jewish company. These were dangerous times.

School days in a grammar school in Frankfurt were by no means happy or easy for Claus. Given his father's comments about the Nazi regime, Claus could not actively support Nazi ideology. His conscience would not permit him to join the Hitler Youth and therefore he tended to be very much an outsider. His lack of enthusiastic support for the regime had consequences:

I was bullied because I was the youngest and the smallest, but there was another dimension – the political. If you were not enthusiastic for the Nazis, you were against them. I therefore found myself doubly bullied. My parents had me removed from the school after the teachers became very negative about my not being an enthusiastic Nazi. I don't think they even realised that I was half-Jewish. I was moved from Wöhlerschule to Musterschule, which was an excellent school. I learned a lot there. We had a superb language teacher, Dr Gerlach, to whom I owe the grounding in English which helped when I came to England. The teacher was able to impart subtleties of the language. He also tried to make us enjoy the English language by giving us Sherlock Holmes stories to read. My grateful thanks to Dr Gerlach.

As a schoolboy walking to school every day, being familiar with the place and the atmosphere, and even though conditions were so hostile under the Nazis, I still felt at home in the circle of my friends. I did not join the Hitler Youth and had to bear the consequences which meant a certain amount of ostracism and all sorts of small but significant factors. To a boy it might mean bullying or being beaten up, but for an older person it might be quite vital because one might lose one's job. Everything in Germany was organised by the Nazi Party and pervaded by its ideology. At school for example, Jewish teachers began to disappear. Nazi teachers took their place and had no hesitation in making propaganda by saying that Jewish financiers are profiteers who had sucked the country dry. I remember one particular fanatical Nazi type going into details of Jews draining Germany of its wealth and then showing off their diamonds in the south of France. In every sphere of life, the Party put people in charge as monitors to make sure that everything happened in line with Nazi policy. Anyone who did not enthusiastically agree with it and support it would disappear or be sidelined. The whole ideology was very pervasive. It was difficult at first as a school boy, not to be swept along by it. It was terribly tempting because as a boy, one wants to conform and be part of the crowd.

On one occasion Claus came very close physically to Adolf Hitler. His school was amongst the crowds on the streets of Frankfurt to greet Hitler's cavalcade, as Claus explains:

I only saw Hitler once in person. It was in 1935 for the opening of the first German Autobahn (motorway) from Frankfurt to Darmstadt. School boys, like myself, and other organisations lined the main road leading to the new autobahn. There I was with everyone else stood in a row as the car with Hitler passed by. He was standing erect in the front passenger seat. The enthusiastic, ecstatic crowd went wild and rushed forward. I was pushed against the door of his car. Hitler was standing just a matter of a few centimetres from my nose, but I wasn't dreadfully impressed and maybe I was already rather prejudiced against him. Here was one of the most powerful leaders in Europe, albeit a tyrant, but he seemed to me like a peasant in his Sunday suit.

The Jews of Germany would receive the brunt of Hitler's virulent anti-Semitism during the 1930s. His book, *Mein Kampf*, written back in 1924 during his imprisonment after the failed Munich 'Beer Hall *putsch*' of 1923, laid the blame for Germany's misfortunes squarely at the feet of the Jews. In all his subsequent speeches he ranted against the Jews whom he identified as war profiteers growing rich while Germans bled. Hand-in-hand with the impressive Nazi uniforms came an ideology which gradually denied Jews and other minority groups their right to exist. In the coming years, the liberties and freedom of those Jews who remained in Germany were gradually eroded. The summer of 1935 saw the passing of the Nuremberg Laws, whereby Jews were no longer allowed to buy goods from Aryan shops or have non-Jewish servants. Neither were they permitted to travel on trams or buses or use public swimming pools and parks. Teaching Hebrew was forbidden and all Jewish passports were withdrawn to be stamped with a red J for *Juden*.

In July 1936, a further flouting of the terms of the Treaty of Versailles occurred when Hitler ordered a massive force of troops to enter the Rhineland. The area had been declared a de-militarised zone under the treaty. The situation for Germany's Jews continued to deteriorate, with acts of brutality against individuals and male Jews disappearing without trace. Jewish shops were boycotted and economic conditions and survival became impossibly hard for most Jewish families. Now in Germany there was a lack of what Claus's father termed 'civil courage'. There *were* those who did not like what was happening under Hitler but turned a blind eye. Curt Ascher now made a point of declaring his solidarity with the Jews. He was an honourable upright man and lived by his moral principles, but it had consequences. An increasing number of his Aryan customers decided not to do business with him. 'He seemed to despair,' comments Claus, 'as though it was no longer worth living under these circumstances and he became quite reckless in what he said and did.' Curt's actions and speech began to worry the young German schoolboy:

> He frightened me on one occasion when we went to a village outside Frankfurt and we were sat in the beer garden. The loud speakers in the trees were spouting forth a political speech and he called the waiter to ask him to turn it off. He said, 'I haven't come here to listen to political speeches.' The waiter turned off the broadcast, but I thought at the time that it was a rather brave thing for my father to have done. It did nothing to take away my unease at his action. There were other times when he did not mind his language and I would tug at his sleeve and say, 'Daddy, be careful!' He looked at me fully in the face and replied: 'do you expect me to act like a coward?'

Although another war was still two years away, Claus's father had read the signs and was open in his views about what Germany was heading for:

> We knew war was coming. Hermann Goering had made the famous 'guns not butter' remark. My father refused to read German newspapers, disgusted by his German nationality. He began to read *The Times* and *Le Temps* which was risky but he considered German papers corrupted by propaganda lies, imposed by Nazi editorial control – with some honourable exceptions. He was somewhat reckless in making his views known. The country had been turned into one of informers. Each apartment block had someone who kept an eye on everyone else (usually the janitor) and would report to the Gestapo about what kind of company their neighbours kept, who visited them and whether they travelled abroad, what kind of mail they received, and whether they read foreign newspapers. The regime frightened people into informing on their neighbours. Conforming was the word of the day. I was increasingly worried by my father's outspokenness. In protest to him, he said something which I have never forgotten:

> *Der eine fragt: was kommt danach? Der Andre: was ist recht? Und darin unterscheidet sich der Ritter von dem Knecht.* This translates as: 'one man asks: what is the

consequence? The other what is right? And therein lies the difference between serf and knight.'

That is the principle by which he lived and by which he died.

From about the age of twelve or thirteen, Claus had joined a Protestant Youth Group *Bibelkreis* (BK) under the leadership of Albert Hamel, a wonderful man with white hair and moustache. 'He was,' says Claus, 'friendly, approachable, full of fun and of high moral standard. He used to give us guidance and pep talks, preaching but without being preachy.' This youth group was not part of the Hitler Youth because it held a different moral standard. As such, it provided an important base from which Claus could cling to his belief that the Nazi regime was wrong. The group was soon banned by the Nazi Party for not conforming to the state ideology:

The group had volunteer helpers, like Rudolf Bien (who later died of pneumonia on the Russian front), Richard Jöst (whose family owned local cafés and was later killed in North Africa as an officer in the Afrika Korps). I had my first ever glass of beer in a Jöst beer garden by the river Main and remember Jöst showing us their ice cream factory. At our weekly meetings Herr Hamel preached a short sermon and read relevant stories. He was a wonderful storyteller and charismatic group leader. He also involved us in instructive question-and-answer sessions and knew how to make our meetings fun and inspiring. He read poetry to us, and one reading made a lasting impression on me. It was of the epic poem entitled *Die Füsse im Feuer* and illustrated one aspect of the principles this group was about. It is about the persecution of Protestants (Huguenots) in sixteenth-century France. When I faced a moral dilemma at the end of the war, this poem gave me the moral answer, but more about that later.

In the youth group we played games, as Cubs or Scouts might do. During the shorter school holidays, Easter and Whitsun, I joined a small group of BK friends who went on hikes. During the long summer holidays there were wonderful summer camps in the Black Forest or the Palatinate. Activities included hikes, excursions, all sorts of games. War games were particularly popular with the group divided into two sections wearing red or blue armbands respectively, each boy equipped with four bamboo spears tipped with corks well upholstered in the section colour. During our skirmishes or battles, if we were hit by an 'enemy' spear, we were considered dead, and had to remove our armband and became a spectator. Richard Jöst proved an excellent section commander.

On one occasion our section was running in single file along a narrow path through the Black Forest undergrowth and there was a small hole in the middle of the path. Our feet pounding over the hole disturbed a wasps' nest with consequences. The first few boys passed unscathed, but I was towards the back of the file and became the target of many angry wasps. My swollen legs took some days to return to normal. On another occasion I spent a couple of holiday weeks at a Protestant youth holiday home. It was connected to a charity actively sponsored by the BK at Bethel near Bielefeld, devoted to caring for disabled children.

Hiking to the summer camps, or the excursions during the shorter school holidays, was a way of getting to know parts of central Germany or the Black Forest quite intimately. During one hot Whitsun holiday we travelled to Mainz and hitched a ride on a tug on the Rhine. We intended to go as far as Linz am Rhein, but as it had no barges in tow we travelled fast downstream. We liked it so much we stayed on it as far as Cologne. On the return journey we were given a lift on one of a barge train being towed upstream, bound for Basel. This travelled much more slowly and took three delightful days back to Mainz. On the first night we stayed over at Remagen, practically under the famous railway bridge. The skipper allowed us to use nails as pegs to erect our small tent on the sloping hatch covers. And when one hot afternoon I fell asleep in it, I woke up as it got cooler towards sundown to find I couldn't move because the tar in the wooden hatch cover had started to solidify and I was stuck fast like Gulliver on the Lilliput beach! When in Frankfurt as a soldier at the end of the war in 1945, I had a re-union with some BK survivors and was also able to visit Albert Hamel and tell him how much the BK had meant to me during these difficult times.

The fun hiking holidays with the Protestant Youth group had their downsides. When Claus returned to school after the long summer holidays he felt very different from his classmates who had attended Hitler Youth camps: 'They had been turned into sharp little Nazis.' The gap between Claus's own upbringing and that of the all-encompassing State ideology was widening:

After a time, when you are stepping out of line, you begin to wonder whether there is something wrong with your own ideology. It was much easier to go along with the certainties of the Nazi Party. Nazism relieved people of the need to think for themselves. It gave certainties. You hand over your responsibility to the Party. It was therefore rather uncomfortable for me as a schoolboy, not to be one of them. It was Nazi policy to make anyone who didn't agree feel that they were on their own. The Youth Group was vitally important to me at the time to find myself amongst like-minded people and not alone. That is why it was later banned. The whole terror of Nazi philosophy was *Gleichschaltung* – unification or conformity.

At the appropriate age, Claus attended confirmation classes run by a tall, good looking and dignified pastor by the name of Wallau. He cut a fine figure and was perhaps a little vain and a bit of an actor which, as Claus comments, 'is not a bad thing for a clergyman'. In due course, the class was confirmed by him. It was at a time when Claus was a member of the BK and rather over-religious as young people tend to be when religion opens up new philosophical and moral perspectives to them. He comments:

In the prevailing circumstances, this may have had an unusual effect on me because one felt very isolated if one was not a party member or supporter. It meant a great deal to be inspired by religious ideals. It was some time later after the BK had been dissolved, that I was walking up the Eckenheimer Landstrasse, a somewhat down-at-heel row of terrace houses. A little way ahead of me a door opened and out strode Pastor Wallau in full officer's uniform, peak cap, shiny boots, white gloves and cape. He strutted down the middle of the road, loving himself. The shock made me feel quite ill. I was allergic to uniforms by then, and the atmosphere in Germany had become ever more stark and bleak. Perhaps I was also outgrowing my religious enthusiasm, but this experience put me off at that instance. Perhaps I was being unjust. He may have been called up to serve in the army like everyone else and become field padre? His theatrical temperament may have enjoyed playing the role. Whatever the facts of the matter, I have rarely been in a church since.

By the beginning of 1937 the Spanish Civil War was well underway. For the Ascher family the hailing of 1937 was spent at the home of Gustav Noske and his wife, little knowing what would befall them that year. Nine months later would see such terrible consequences of Curt Ascher's outspoken politics against the regime. At that evening dinner, Claus vividly remembers his embarrassment at having burnt a hole in house-proud Frau Noske's damask tablecloth! He comments, 'I did not own up to it, and nothing was said.'

In September 1937 Claus's mother travelled to Bremen to visit her brother and other relatives. Claus, now fifteen, remained in Frankfurt with his father. One day they went out together to the Römerberg, a cobbled square lined with fine fifteenth-century half-timbered houses in the old part of Frankfurt, birthplace of Goethe. What began as a quiet harmless supper turned into a nightmare:

We were eating our sausage and sauerkraut and chatting to each other, with others around long rustic tables. The conversation turned to the new stories about Spain and the situation in the Bay of Biscay. A recent news item had reported about two German battlecruisers, *Scharnhorst* and *Gneisenau*, that were said to be on manoeuvres in the Bay of Biscay. 'That's nonsense,' said my father. 'They are bombing north Spanish towns and helping the rebel General Franco against the democratically elected government.' Father's comment put a damper on things around our table. An American citizen of German extraction who was a customer impressed by the Nazi power with its flags and soldiers marching to military songs turned to my father and made a comment. My father replied to him, 'Look under the surface and where this is all leading.' And again it put a damper on the conversation.

A young man at the table then got up and disappeared. He returned with a policeman and pointed to my father. The policeman beckoned to my father and off he went. I waited for quite some time drinking the rest of my beer, our dog at my feet and my father's walking stick against the table. I waited and waited, getting ever more concerned and fearful. Eventually a police inspector came along and paid the bill. He then spoke to me and asked me to accompany him. I was taken to the nearby police station where my father was now under arrest. In a typical German gesture of looking over both shoulders before talking in case someone was listening, the police inspector said to me, 'how could he say such things? Doesn't he know how dangerous it is to talk like that nowadays?' We arrived at the police station where I saw my father. The first thing he did was to thrust some papers at me with the gesture to 'tuck these in your pocket.' The police officer on duty was watching us and reacted immediately, 'what are those papers? I'll have those.' My father replied, 'Oh, only copies of private letters.' They were indeed private letters but of a political nature with people's names on them, so it was vital that they did not fall into the wrong hands. I then left my father, took the dog and his stick back home.

Claus's mother Mathilde managed to see her husband twice whilst he was in 'protective custody'. She was told that he was being held for 'his own protection'. During her visit, they talked about mundane things. Curt then said to her, 'It's getting towards the end of summer, could you bring me my winter suit and mend the sleeve lining?' Mathilde replied, 'What sleeve lining?' He pretended to be impatient, 'If I've told you once, I've told you a dozen times, the sleeve lining wants mending.' As they kissed goodbye he whispered, 'That sleeve lining is important.' When Mathilde returned home, she went through his suits together with Claus and they found rolled up documents in the sleeves of various jackets. 'That evening,' says Claus, 'we had a bonfire in our living room. It wasn't safe to burn the documents outside in the garden.' The next time Mathilde went to see Curt she was able to reassure him that she had mended the sleeve lining. That was the last time she saw him. Claus recalls:

I only saw him once at Gestapo Headquarters before he was taken to Dachau. There was an alcove with benches, the officer opened various doors and out came my father being taken down the stairs by two Gestapo officers. He was not in very good shape. We had no opportunity to exchange conversation. And that was the last time that I saw him.

Curt was handed over to the Gestapo and transported to Dachau concentration camp, 7km north-west of Munich.

Curt Ascher's name is listed in the *Zugangsbücher* (intake-books) which are now held at the National Archives and Record Administration in Washington D.C. The entry shows that he was born on 12 December 1882 in Glatz-Oberschlesien and imprisoned in Dachau on 2 October 1937, registered under prisoner number 12792. Dachau was the first of the concentration camps to be opened in 1933 on Hitler's instructions, initially for political prisoners who were kept there in 'protective custody'. Surrounded by a barbed wire electric fence with watchtowers and moat, inside the complex consisted of stark lines of huts, a parade ground and disinfectant hut for clothing. It had a prison ('bunker'), prison yard and whitewashed wall against which many prisoners were shot. The camp was run on a strict brutal daily schedule with harsh punishments for the slightest infraction.

After the pogrom known as *Kristallnacht* (the Night of Broken Glass) the following year, tens of thousands of Jews were incarcerated in Dachau. It was set up to act as a deterrent to scare the German people into submission to the Nazi ideology. The commandant Theodor Eicke ran a brutal regime under squads of SS death head units. During its functioning years until liberation in April 1945, over 200,000 prisoners were incarcerated in the camp. At least 30,000 officially died there, although the figures are probably higher since many deaths went unrecorded. Until 1938, most like Curt were political prisoners of the state, communists and Social Democrats. The day after his arrival, Curt sent a postcard to his wife and son from Dachau, postmarked 3 October 1937. Translated from the original German it reads:

My dearest ones, after a long journey I arrived here and have already settled in somewhat. I am in good health and you need not worry about me. Please send at once money which is vitally important here because I must obtain a pair of glasses and various other things. It is permitted to send 15 Mark a week. Please send this each week. Your father.

Just one further piece of correspondence was sent from the concentration camp – a letter postmarked Dachau and dated 10 October 1937. One page of it survives intact, however the second page has been censored by the Nazis by being cut down the middle, such that only half can be read. Claus has kept it in his possession and it has been reproduced as an illustration in the centre of this biography. It reads:

> My very dear ones, all mail addressed to me must show a sender on the envelope and written in ink. I am in good health but am terribly worried since I have not heard from you while all the others who came at the same time as I have already heard from home. Please make it your absolute rule to settle everything about which I asked immediately because otherwise I have to assume the worst about you. Now I have not heard since 13 September. I don't know how the problem of the apartment, etc has been solved. Also you wrote in that letter that the extremely important 5 Mark payments have in the meantime been increased.[5] These payments are more important than food and drink and are the most...'
>
> [The letter is not legible hereafter because it has been cut in half.]

That was the last correspondence received from Claus's father. Five days later, on 15 October 1937, Curt died in Dachau. The circumstances surrounding his death and the cause of death were never given. During the research for this biography, contact was made with the archivist at Dachau, and although there is an entry in a ledger for Curt's death, there is no record of the cause of death. A Gestapo officer subsequently called at the Ascher home and informed Mathilde and Claus that he had died:

> Maybe the Gestapo officer told us, or I saw it written somewhere, but I seem to recall that the cause of death was given as circulation failure. Whether that was the truth, I will never know. At the time, deaths were still dealt with on an individual basis and so some of my father's personal belongings were returned to us. To this day I have kept the list of items that were sent back to us. It wasn't yet the industrialised mass murders and extermination programme that was in place from 1942, but it was still a ruthless and brutal elimination of opposition and of people who didn't fit in. Of course, the Jews were very high on that list. We were never told how my father died. My mother and I went to Munich to establish whether we could still see him before the funeral, but the SS said that it could not be done. We were allowed to attend the cremation, which we did. My father's ashes were then posted to us in an urn through the regular mail. We even had to pay the postage.

Curt Ascher's ashes were interred in the Jewish cemetery Frankfurt North. The funeral oration was given by Rabbi Salzberger in which he spoke of Curt's 'golden laughter and high principles'. He then proceeded to describe him as: '*Ein Ritter ohne Furcht und Tadel*', and '*Chevalier sans Peur et sans Reproche*' – a knight without fear and beyond reproach. It was a fitting epitaph.

Life for Claus changed immediately after his father's death: 'I was still at school when my father died. There was constant tension and fear. We were very hard up. I left school straightaway because there were school fees to be paid at the grammar school. I never did very well anyway and was always surprised to pass from form to form. Every year I fully expected not to make it and to have to repeat a year.' Initially, Claus's mother lived off public welfare and private charity from her brother. Later she tried to earn money as best she could. For some time she worked for the post office, loading and unloading mail bags at Frankfurt East railway station, taking cover in the air raid shelter when there was time or sheltering as best she could, until she was summarily dismissed as she 'had been married to a Jew and didn't even get divorced!' She was later re-instated after appeal, but to a different department.

Frau Else Wüst became an important figure to Claus and his mother at this time. She was no Nazi and had been a police inspector before being dismissed, presumably for not conforming. At the time of Curt's death she was practising as a physiotherapist-masseuse and welfare worker and aided Claus and his mother. She made it possible for remittances from Claus's uncle Hans in Bremen to be transmitted through her channels to his mother. And it was she who was eventually instrumental in getting Claus out of Germany. It was not an easy relationship: 'She was inclined to be rather domineering and acrid,' comments Claus, 'but I would never say anything bad about her because I owe her my life. She started the proceedings and made the definite decision that I had to get out of Germany.' Having had to leave school, Claus took up an apprenticeship as a commercial apprentice to the Frankfurt Asbestos Works at Niederrad, on the outskirts of Frankfurt:

I used to cycle to Niederrad every morning. I didn't learn an awful lot there, but it was a good environment to be in. I developed a sharp instinct of whom you could talk to and whom you did not. You could feel who was a Nazi type or a nationalist, or someone who hesitated to join the Nazi mentality. You learn to 'smell' a Social Democrat. That applied to the employees of the asbestos works. I attended evening classes and learnt typing. In about 1935, I had been allowed to join a Jewish sports club called the *Schild*, the 'Shield'. I was in the fencing section and quickly learned how to use the foil, etc. It was led by Gerd Blumenfeld whose family owned the Frankfurt asbestos works where I eventually got a job. The asbestos works was sold under duress to a Nazi-approved buyer who continued to run the business. The Blumenfeld family immigrated to the USA with what money was left after most of the proceeds of the sale were paid in *Reichsfluchtsteuer*.

By the autumn of 1938, war looked inevitable, even though on the diplomatic stage Britain was still trying to negotiate with Germany. In September 1938, British Prime Minister Neville Chamberlain flew to Germany to have face-to-face talks with Adolf Hitler at the Petersberg Hotel on the Rhine not far from the city of Bonn. During their conference, the two leaders discussed the crisis over the Sudetenland. At the end of the month, on 30 September, they signed the Munich Agreement. Chamberlain returned to Britain with high expectations of having averted another world war and promised 'peace in our time'. Britain was not ready for another conflict, the memories of the horrors of the First World War and the loss of millions of lives still deeply affected the nation.

Whilst Chamberlain returned from Germany with renewed optimism, the already dire situation for Germany's Jews was deteriorating at an alarming rate. In early November 1938, fourteen months after Curt Ascher's death in Dachau, the Nazis unleashed *Kristallnacht*. Throughout Germany and Austria not a single Jewish family or community would be untouched by its consequences. On 7 November 1938, German diplomat Ernst vom Rath was shot in Paris by Polish Jew Herschel Grynszpan in retaliation for the deportation of his family to Zbuczyn, a border town in the Polish corridor between Germany and Poland. Rath lay in a critical condition in a French hospital. Two days later he died from his wounds. That day also marked the fifteenth anniversary of Hitler's failed 1923 *Putsch* (coup) in Munich. The death of vom Rath was *the* trigger Hitler was waiting for to carry out a tirade of violence against the Jews. During the night of 9–10 November, the Jews of Germany and Austria paid a heavy price for Grynszpan's action. In cities across Germany and Austria, synagogues were set on fire, the windows of Jewish businesses were smashed with shards of glass littering the pavements, shops looted and their buildings torched. Throughout Germany and Austria over a thousand synagogues were destroyed that night, many now burnt-out shells of their former glory. Germany had not seen such destruction against its Jews in the five years since Hitler had come to power back in 1933. Although Claus was not Jewish, his family's political views meant that he was increasingly at risk in these dangerous times. He witnessed that terrible night in Frankfurt:

> In the German press it was reported as a spontaneous uprising against Jews, but it was obvious to everyone that it was not spontaneous because people were delegated to certain areas to attack Jewish businesses, institutions, synagogues, and to arrest Jewish males. *Kristallnacht* wasn't a great surprise

because we were used to things getting worse, but it was an eye-opener. It was a distinctive step in things becoming more brutal. Now the propaganda machine under Goebbels no longer tried to misrepresent things or hide their brutality. They didn't even try to lie convincingly in the German press anymore. If you saw anything, you kept quiet and increasingly wore blinkers. It was what had disgusted my father more than anything else whilst he was alive – the lack of civil courage in the German population. Sticking your neck out, even if you hadn't done anything criminal was not a good idea. If you were noticed, then you could get into deep trouble without knowing what it was for. It didn't matter. So long as people were brutalised or even killed, others toed the line.

In the words of Edmund Burke (1729–97): 'All that is necessary for evil to triumph is for good men to do nothing.' As Claus returned home from work that evening, he saw the full scale of the destruction. As it got dark, the scene was very dramatic. Thick black smoke with a red-tinged glow filled the air, the fire brigade called out but standing by to ensure that the premises of Aryans were not affected. The West End Synagogue in Frankfurt was destroyed that night, where Claus had belonged to its cultural life: arts and music. It was here that he was part of the organisation called the Jewish Kulturbund, even though he was not Jewish. It had been formed to offer culture and art to the liberal minded and provide employment for Jewish artists who were prevented from performing. The Kulturbund Orchestra comprised of many leading instrumentalists, among them Felix Robert Mendelssohn. Claus was not a member of the Kulturbund Orchestra, but attended their concerts. Mendelssohn became a great friend and frequent visitor of Claus's parents when his father was alive. Claus began to take cello lessons with Mendelssohn, who felt he had great potential and no small amount of talent. 'My parents had bought me a cello,' he recalls, 'but unfortunately later in the war the RAF came and burnt my cello in Frankfurt!' Claus joined a small youth orchestra made up of Mendelssohn's pupils along with other young students of the violin and viola. Frankfurt's West End Synagogue was the venue where they rehearsed. Mendelssohn was already a well-known concert cellist and conductor and had founded the Mendelssohn Quartet. Claus also attended a youth group which Mendelssohn had established for his pupils. However, Mendelssohn immigrated to America and rapidly became part of the music scene there. His distinguished career led to his appointment as professor in the Faculty of Music at New York University.

The lives of friends of the Aschers were also affected by what was happening in Germany. News eventually got back to Claus's mother that her friend Mrs Pariser from Bad Homburg had been targeted by the Nazis on *Kristallnacht*:

She was a very good woman who did a lot of good work in Bad Homburg. She continued to maintain friendship with my mother after we left the town. We were told by another acquaintance that whilst they were walking in Bad Homburg behind two SA men, they overheard their conversation. One said to the other: 'I've been told to go to Frau Pariser's flat and smash it up, but I'm not going to do it because she's a very good woman. She has done so much fine work.' On this occasion, the SA man did not agree with what he had been ordered to do on *Kristallnacht*. In her last letter to my mother, Else Pariser said goodbye as she was now going to take her life to forestall deportation, and hoped that under prevailing circumstances mother would understand and not hold it against her.

No crystal ball was needed to see what lay ahead. Claus's days in Germany were numbered. Emigration looked to be the only possible chance of survival:

Political opponents and Jews were being treated with increasing brutality. The situation in Germany had deteriorated so much that it became ever more obvious that if I was not prepared, or able, to join what was going on in Germany I would have to get out.

By now the daily queues outside the embassies and legations in Germany reached right around the block. Desperate émigrés clung to the hope that they would be one of the lucky ones. The Nazis had made it exceptionally difficult for Jews and other émigrés to leave the country. For many, it became a bureaucratic nightmare, by which time any immigration quotas into countries they wanted to go were already allocated:

Many people left it much too late to leave Nazi Germany. It seems strange given what we know now of the Holocaust. Why didn't people leave the country whilst they still could? The reason – they felt German; they *were* German, their families had been Germans for generations. They were respected citizens, born and brought up in Germany and their parents had fought for Germany in the First World War. It did not occur to them that atrocities would be committed against their own people. From what I observed at the time Jews, in particular, seemed to be in denial about what was brewing. Even Sigmund Freud in Vienna had not believed the regime would last in 1938. Many Jews left it too late to decide to leap into the dark and move to a foreign country; and by the time they did, it was already very late and the Nazis had put more obstacles in the way of emigration. Life became impossible for Jewish people and it became practically impossible to emigrate anymore. The first application was always to America.

The Americans welcomed refugees with open arms, but they were not all to come at once. America had national, annual quotas which for Germans and Austrians were already oversubscribed. Therefore names, including mine, were put on a waiting list. My number issued by the American Consulate in Stuttgart was 24132. At that time I was living at 9 Lersnerstrasse, Frankfurt-am-Main. I suppose my number would have come up in 1956 or something by which time it would have been too late for me.

All efforts were focused on trying to get Claus out of Germany. It was the Quakers who came to his aid, as they did for many whose lives were in danger under the Nazis:

> I was put in touch with vicar of the English Church in Frankfurt and it was through him and the Quakers that the necessary guarantee was given for my emigration to Britain. I had to have paperwork to show that I would not be a financial burden to the state. The British approach to emigration was different from the American one. The British policy effectively said, that although it is a tiny island and can't accept immigrants, however if it is a matter of saving your life, then we will issue a transit visa on the understanding that you will go on to America when your number comes up.

With his name on the waiting list for America, Claus and his mother proceeded to visit the vicar of the English Church. Claus can remember that day vividly:

> He had a comfortable flat with rather deep armchairs. It was the cheerfully informal attitude as expressed in the way he bowled the globular cigarette lighter over the carpet. It is strange how I remember semi-irrelevant snapshots at a time when in reality my life was in danger. Although I do not remember his name, that vicar was one link in the chain of events and kindness before I left Germany and it was he who saved my life. Because my father had died in a concentration camp, I was increasingly at risk, something of which I only became gradually aware.

Frau Else Wüst continued to support the family in a number of ways and had some hand in securing Claus's emigration to England. Having been accepted by the Quakers, it took some weeks to get the right stamps and authorisation on papers to leave Germany. It was a tense time: 'You never really knew what lay around the corner whilst you waited for the paperwork to be completed. It was an anxious time and often a bureaucratic nightmare.'

In that waiting period before Claus left Germany, he met a small group of communists through a friend. They were a group of young people who happened to be communists. They met to have coffee together or had discussions in one of their homes. They were under surveillance by the Nazis and Claus remembers opening a window quite late one night. In the pitch darkness under a lamp post there was a butcher's boy with striped apron, standing by his bicycle with basket in front. He was waiting in the shadows, but Claus saw him. He was evidently not delivering meat at midnight, but was Gestapo and was keeping note of who was gathered and when they were there: 'We would raise our glasses to him and make a joke of it. We did not aim to achieve anything radical, but we did commit some symbolic acts against the regime.' Those acts included Claus handing over his father's pistol to the group because they were collecting arms and hiding them. The leader of the group was called Holzl. One day he precariously climbed over the railing of a balcony to remove a loose brick, behind which he had plans of the fortress Ehrenbreitstein opposite Mainz on the Rhine. What a foreign power should do, or be able to do, with plans of this kind was unclear, but at least the lads felt that they were doing their bit:

> It was not about heroics but more a statement to ourselves. The group fulfilled the role which for me had previously been played by the BK (the Protestant Youth Group). It *was* a rather dangerous thing to do, but I was in danger anyway. It was much more important for moral encouragement to be with like-minded people and to feel that you were stating your case. It was a matter of self-esteem and in that respect it made a huge difference psychologically. That was essential given what we were living under.

CHAPTER 3

Emigration

Four days before Christmas 1938, Claus's mother signed a declaration paving the way for her son to leave Germany. It read: 'I hereby declare myself in agreement with the emigration of my son Claus Ascher.'[6] That same day a certificate arrived in the post from the Hitler Youth (*Banne und Jungbanne* 81/186) as part of the paperwork required for Claus to leave Germany: 'It is hereby certified that Claus Ascher, non-Aryan, Frankfurt-am-Main, Lersnerstrasse 9, is not a member of the Hitler Youth.'[7] The amount chargeable for the issuing of the document was 7 marks. These were just one of a number of certificates and paperwork needed to obtain a passport for emigration. In December 1938 Claus received the *Unbedenklichkeitsbescheinigung*, the statement of no impediment, confirming that he owed nothing to the State.[8] The British consulate-general in Frankfurt wrote a letter to him, which reads in translation from the original German:

For the purpose of submission to the appropriate German authorities I hereby certify that I am prepared to issue you with a visa for entry into England as soon as you are in possession of a valid passport. This certificate will be issued in duplicate to prisoners. One original is to be submitted to the Gestapo together with the application for release. The other original is for submission together with the application for a passport to the Passport Office. This certificate is valid for Mr Claus Ascher.

With his name still on the waiting list for America, Claus was finally issued with a German passport and a visa to enter Britain. The visa sent in duplicate: 'this was in case you were taken to a concentration camp,' he comments, 'and needed the second copy to get out.' Claus's mother received a letter from the Jewish Welfare Association in Frankfurt, originally in German: 'We hereby inform you that your son Claus, who has a guarantor, will be attached to the transport which will take place on Tuesday 7th of this month to England.'[9] Now nothing stood in the way of emigration. Being aged over sixteen, Claus was too old to be officially part of the Kindertransport, however age was not the only reason:

> The reason for my being attached was not only my age, but that I had not been adopted by a British foster family under the Kindertransport scheme, but been granted a transit visa to enter Britain on the strength of my US immigration waiting number. I was under guarantee provided by the Quakers on the understanding that I would move on to the USA when the number came up. The annual quota for German-born applicants for immigration into the USA in the late 1930s was about 25,000, but in any case open only to those who could provide a sponsor to guarantee that they would not become a charge on the state. This guarantee was provided for me by my half-sister, Suzanne Stahl, daughter of my father's first marriage, dissolved before the First World War, who had married an American. She was widowed and living in the USA which enabled the US Consulate at Stuttgart to include me in the waiting list for German born applicants under No.24132.

With an uncertain future ahead, the time came for him to say goodbye to his mother:

> My mother had already suffered enough with the death of father and subsequent financial hardship. Now she faced losing me but she truly believed that I would have the chance of a normal existence elsewhere. I said farewell to her at home because it wasn't desirable to have emotional scenes at the railway station. I asked her not to come to the station with me. I left home armed with only a small suitcase, the contents of which had been listed by my mother, a list which I have still kept to this day. We were required to carry an inventory of what was being taken out of Germany in case we were checked by SS en route.

On 6 February 1939, just days before his seventeenth birthday, Claus took a tram to the main train station in Frankfurt to join a Kindertransport out of Germany. It was a critical time because on reaching the age of seventeen, he would have become liable for military service under German universal conscription. It would have 'put further obstacles in the way of my emigration and made life more difficult for my mother'. Inside Frankfurt station he joined a group of children under the charge of Mr Blaschke. He coped almost superficially, suggesting there was 'an element of excited anticipation of the journey and the great adventure of going abroad. Maybe that was to protect myself from the real emotional trauma at this time.' Claus, along with the children, boarded a train destined for the Hook of Holland. The journey was not uneventful. There were some difficult moments:

When we came to the frontier station at Emmerich, the SS guards decided to play a psychological game with us. We were all ordered off the train and told to leave on the gravel side of the ballast between the two pairs of rails (not the platform side). It was quite a height to jump, especially for the younger children. The SS guards scattered our suitcases and the contents about the track. They proceeded to cut in half the tie of one youngster in case he was hiding currency in it. It was forbidden to export any foreign currency. The SS men were generally unpleasant and then one of them said: 'none of you can leave. You're all staying here. You're not going.' At that moment everyone's heart sank to their boots. We really believed that we would not get out of Germany. And then just before the train left they ordered us to get back on the train. There was hurried stuffing of belongings back into suitcases and lifting them up to the floor of the carriage. We clambered up and collapsed in our seats, exhausted by the stress and tension. Literally seconds later the train began to slide out of Emmerich station. Then after we had tried to recover a bit from the shock, the compartment door was flung open by Mr Blaschke who shouted: '*Wir sind auf holländischem Boden!*' (We are on Dutch soil!) This sudden explosive relief of tension was about as much as one could bear. I nearly fainted and felt sick. I had not been aware of the constant pressure and tension that I had been living under for all these years and to have it suddenly relieved like that was a bit like a diver coming up too quickly and suffering the bends when the pressure is suddenly released. It was an amazing feeling to be free and gradually we began to breathe and realise that it was all over. Nazi Germany was well behind us.

The train eventually pulled into the large station at Rotterdam. It provided Claus with another reminder of how normality here was different from Nazi Germany. It was evening rush hour, the station was crowded. Some platforms had small trains waiting to depart on local rail networks:

On these crowded platforms people were looking at this train full of children with compassion in their faces. It was a shock. The Germans didn't do compassion at the time. To see people who had hearts, who looked at us knowing full well what we had come from, it was the most moving experience for me.

Finally the train arrived at the Hook of Holland. The émigré children and Claus boarded a boat bound for Harwich in England. After the night crossing, the boat docked in the early hours of the morning. Claus was about to set foot for the first time in his life on English soil. The issue of identity for refugees entering the country was complex at this time:

> I arrived on a German passport and was admitted to Britain as a German national on a transit visa. I was considered to be a German national even much later when I was in the army. The Germans considered me deprived of my German nationality, but the British still regarded me as a German national.

What were his first impressions of England?

> It was a culture shock. Everything was rather strange and smelt different. We piled into what seemed to me to be funny little English trains compared to the big German *Reichsbahn* trains. Unlike German trains, the small English train was very comfortable with upholstered seats. The carriages smelt of thick cigarette aroma and their windows plastered with transparent advertisements for cigarettes. The train started moving, and much to our surprise, went at a hell of a pace. It may have been small and toy-like in some ways compared to German trains, but it could certainly go some speed.

From Harwich, the train sped through the unfamiliar English countryside. Claus took it all in, barely believing that he was now free. 'The train eventually pulled into the incredible disorganised welter of London's Liverpool Street station which was,' he comments, 'in complete contrast to the orderly methodical German stations. I was greeted with enormous sympathy and warmth by the British people.' On the platform, a Quaker lady was waiting to greet him. She then took him into the centre of the city to a small hotel in Woburn Place area. Soon it was time for something to eat:

> She took me to a Lyons' Corner House for a meal which impressed me enormously. They were to be found all over London and were very popular. Inside there was an orchestra playing good classical music, the musicians all dressed in red tailcoats. Some of them were continental refugees no doubt! It all seemed to me very luxurious and friendly. Later that evening when we returned to the hotel, looking out of the window at night, what struck me most was the enormous number of chimneys. As far as the eye could see were roofs full of chimneys to accommodate the English custom of a fire in every room. In Germany we were not used to having a fireplace in every room. We had

central heating. These were my first impressions of London. The following day, the Quaker lady took me on a sight-seeing tour of the city to see such places as the British Museum. The whole experience was overwhelming and numbed me to a degree.

Claus had come to Britain, like many young men, on a transit visa. The next day the Quaker lady accompanied him to the Wallingford Farm Training Colony, just outside Wallingford in Berkshire. The centre was run by the Christian Service Union for approximately two hundred children who came from a disadvantaged family or were homeless. All were being trained for a career in agriculture. With several hundred acres of land, the farm had cows and horses. Claus was to train as a market gardener. The centre was organised pretty much along the lines of an English public school. There were four houses, each headed by a House Master and House Mistress. The children were each allocated to one of the houses:

I was in Albright House which was headed by House Master Capt. Napier. He was a very understanding man. He was a descendant of General Sir Charles Napier, erstwhile commander-in-chief, who later inherited the baronetcy. A good man, who devoted his retirement to serve the interests of disadvantaged children. He was called House Father; Captain and Mrs. Napier were the house parents of Albright House. Although the training farm was so different from my background, it did not feel strange. Under the circumstances I didn't feel like questioning what was happening. One was glad to accept what fate offered. I liked many of the boys there. We went out to the little copses, chopping wood, and I remember learning how to load a dung cart properly so it doesn't all slide down again. I did not automatically take to market gardening as a natural, but I felt at home. There was Mr Drinkwater, known to us as 'Drinkie', who had served in the First World War. He was the under-gardener under Mr. Lye and liked to air such words of French as he remembered from his time on the Western Front. He was a very considerate man. The boys may not always have treated him with respect, but they did regard him with great affection. I learnt quite a lot from him. I remember the Glacier mints with which he was very generous in handing out. I was part of a nice companionable group. When it rained, we took shelter and chatted. We were almost a family.

The training farm was run along lines of rather old-fashioned discipline, such that occasionally a boy might be caned. There was a *6d* weekly pocket money. We were strictly not allowed to swear. That was demonstrated one day when one boy I rather liked was putting up a notice. He kept hitting his thumb and got rather irritated. Finally he drove in the last nail with a volley of 'bugger, bugger, bugger, bugger, bugger'. That cost him *30d*.

A new wing was soon established at the colony for the arrival of refugee boys. Claus was sent off to visit refugee transit camps like the Kitchener Camp, near Sandwich in Kent, where some boys were being housed temporarily.[10] His brief was to talk to them about agricultural training and to recruit them:

> I had a briefing from Sir Stead in Woburn Square, London, then went on my way to the various camps, including Kitchener Camp. I drew a resounding zero! The boys were mainly townies who were absolutely not interested in agriculture or land work. I returned to the training farm with a sense of failure. I soon discovered that the boys were sent to us anyway. An assignment of wooden huts arrived which we had to assemble ourselves under supervision. That became the refugee wing of the Wallingford Farm Training Colony. I was initially head boy for the refugees but I took the role too seriously and tried to represent the boys in every respect, and made myself a bit unpopular. Eventually someone else was installed as head boy.

Over the summer of 1939 the clouds of war were looming:

> War seemed inevitable. Nothing could turn the tide, except a miracle. We were hoping for war as a resolution of something that was not going to be solved any other way. My heart was in favour of the Allies, and opposed to Nazi Germany which had to be defeated. By the time Hitler invaded Poland, there was never any question about whose side I was on. My father had come to admire England and its values, read *The Times* rather than German papers. I found his and the general world-wide admiration of, and respect for, British values were amply confirmed by the way in which I was received here. What impressed me was that in general, people were happy to accept me at face value as an anti-Nazi of German nationality. With the approach of war, we noticed that people were already being called up for service.

Adolf Hitler did not heed British Prime Minister Chamberlain's warning about invading Poland. On 1 September, in defiance of European opinion, Hitler marched into Poland and incorporated it into the Greater Reich. Chamberlain kept his promise that if Hitler did so, Britain would declare war on Germany. On 3 September 1939, Claus sat by the radio set with others on the farm to listen to Chamberlain's broadcast to the nation:

> I am speaking to you from No. 10 Downing Street. This morning the British Ambassador in Berlin handed the German government a final note, stating that unless the British government heard from them by 11 o'clock that they were

prepared at once to withdraw their troops from Poland, a state of war would exist between us. I have to tell you now that no such undertaking has been received and that consequently this country is at war with Germany.

Britain was now at war with Claus's former country: 'It was no great shock. When it did come, it was a relief. It was evidently clear that Hitler had to be got rid of.' Across Britain thousands of refugees from Nazi oppression, like Claus, found their status had changed overnight. They were now classified by the British government as 'enemy aliens'.

Claus was about to be sent to the Eddisbury Fruit Farm at Kelsall, Chester, belonging to Mr L. Haworth who was related to Mrs Adelaide McGowan-Priori, the Quaker lady who had made it possible for him to come to England. It was intended to start him on his future career, but this was frustrated at the last moment by a case of diphtheria at the colony which caused it to be placed under quarantine. During November 1939, Claus moved from the Wallingford Farm Training Colony to an elegant house in the country at Crowmarsh. The head gardener at the Wallingford Farm Training Colony wrote the following reference of recommendation for him:

This is to certify that C. Ascher has worked here on the gardens from Feb 1939 – Nov 1939. During that period he has taken a keen interest in his work which consisted vegetable and flower cultivation, lawns and fruit. I have always found him honest, willing & obliging.[11]

Claus was to work as garden boy but found himself unsuccessful. Few memories remain for him of this particular period at Crowmarsh. Only one incident sticks in his mind when the lady of the house, Mrs Newby-Robson, conscious of his original background, asked him: 'And what about you?' She was concerned about his trustworthiness as a German. Whose side was he on? There was understandable concern about the possibility of fifth columnists (spies), but Claus was more than conscious that this was his war. Until his eighteenth birthday, on 13 February 1940, he was not old enough to volunteer for the British forces.

In the late spring of 1940 events across the English Channel were moving at a rapid pace. On 9 April, Hitler's forces crossed into Denmark virtually unopposed. A month later, on 10 May, Nazi troops swept into Belgium, Holland and France breaking through the Allied lines, cutting off Dunkirk and trapping the British Expeditionary Force. Paris was declared an open city. That same day, 10 May 1940, the sixty-five-year-old Winston Churchill drove to Buckingham Palace to ask the King's permission to form a new government after the resignation of Neville Chamberlain. It was to be a significant day for the British people because

Churchill's appointment would be Britain's salvation. His strong leadership would bring the country through its darkest hour. He was quick to react to news from Europe and ordered the immediate evacuation of some 300,000 troops from the beaches around Dunkirk in an epic rescue operation. With much of Europe now under Nazi control, Britain was next on Hitler's agenda, as captured intelligence later proved. The country braced itself and began preparing coastal defences in a hurried attempt to prevent an invasion.

Now there was a real fear that fifth columnists would be parachuted into Britain as they had been in Norway. Churchill's attention turned to the refugees living in this country. They could be infiltrated and it would be virtually impossible to tell who was a genuine refugee from Nazi oppression. As a matter of security, Churchill was advised to intern those of enemy nationality, the so-called 'enemy aliens'. Up and down the country, thousands of Germans, Austrians and Italians received a knock on the door from a policeman in the early hours of the morning and were arrested. During May and June 1940, nearly 30,000 were interned behind barbed wire in Churchill's policy of 'collar the lot'. They remained in internment for several months, sometimes longer, while Parliament debated their situation. The majority were interned on the Isle of Man, living in requisitioned hotels and boarding houses behind barbed wire. It was here that the camps became a microcosm of Central European intellect, with the formation of a mini university, an orchestra and the Amadeus Quartet. Artists, sculptors, scientists, musicians, doctors, surgeons and professors organised lectures and cultural activities.

Meanwhile, around 1,500 internees were put aboard the *SS Arandora Star* bound for Canada. On 2 July the ship was torpedoed by a German U-boat off the coast of Ireland, resulting in loss of life. The survivors were pulled from the freezing waters and taken back to internment camps. A few days later they joined 2,000 other internees on the troopship *Dunera* at Liverpool, bound for Australia. The *Dunera* sailed on 10 July 1940, also carrying 251 Nazi POWs and 200 Italian Fascists, all Category A prisoners and deemed a threat to national security. The internees suffered a nine-week journey to Sydney amidst appalling conditions on board. Many likened the *Dunera* to a floating concentration camp. Whilst all this was going on for other enemy aliens, Claus was spared internment for much of that summer. 'There was also a certain amount of randomness about the whole internment policy. I was just lucky, I suppose.' He believes it was because there was a shortage of staff at the Wallingford Farm Training Colony as they had been called up to fight. Claus was engaged as one of the welfare officers.

Claus had kept in regular touch with his mother until the outbreak of war when all direct communications ceased. He worried about her fate left behind in Germany; his only consolation was that she was a Protestant (unlike his father) and would have some measure of protection from the Nazis, although he knew that ultimately she may have no protection from the Allied bombers:

Each of us kept a numbered register to keep track of letters and acknowledgements. Until the war, mother had kept me abreast of the way she tried to keep her head above water and about conditions in Germany getting more difficult all the time. She also kept me updated about friends. Some of them helped her a great deal and gave sorely needed moral support in those difficult days. In spite of her struggle for existence and many problems, her letters often took the form of 'No Commercial Value' packets containing touching and thoughtful gifts like cigarettes, gloves, socks she had knitted and the like – and always, if available, International Reply Coupons to save me the cost of postage in spite of her very straitened circumstances. She eked out a living by taking on typing work and other poorly paid jobs including (I learnt after the war) as a post office worker. At first she was in the small packet sorting department. It was from this work that she was summarily dismissed on the grounds of 'having been married to a Jew, and not even having taken steps to divorce him!' She was later re-instated on appeal, though demoted to loading and unloading mailbags on Frankfurt East station. Very heavy work, often interrupted by running for the shelter during air raids, or a tunnel full of pipework if there was no time to reach the shelter when being strafed by low-flying aircraft.

When war broke out, direct mail communication ceased, but we were still able to exchange letters through my sister Suzanne in America so long as the USA remained neutral. This was of course slower and more infrequent, and had to be phrased with care because of the German censorship of all foreign mail. Fortunately, she had the support of good friends who took the risk of befriending a politically suspect person. There were friends from my days with the BK, a Catholic family whom she used to join in processions out of solidarity, and a number of others. Gustav and Ina Lenzewski were enormously supportive and Mrs Pariser at Bad Homburg was a particularly good and kind person.

Britain stood alone in opposing the might of the Nazi war machine. In the skies above southern England, the Battle of Britain pilots fought courageously. By now Claus had become increasingly conscious of wanting to play his part in the downfall of Hitler. He knew only too well the brutality of the regime from his own experience and the fate of his father in Dachau. He wanted to fight. On 11 September 1940, he wrote to the American Consulate General to say that he was volunteering for the Auxiliary Military Pioneer Corps, a labour corps of the British army, but the only unit open at that time to 'enemy aliens'. Claus had been advised that he was still entitled to retain his name on the waiting list for immigration to the United States. In between this letter and his next to the Consulate, dated 19 October 1940, it is clear that his name had been placed on the 'inactive list of persons waiting allotment of German quota numbers'. In writing to the American Consulate on 19 October, he requested an urgent interview. His reasons, given in that letter, are enlightening. Here was a man who felt he had an obligation to fight the Nazis:

> … whether there are any possibilities for me to join the American army, as I am informed that a conscription law has been passed in the United States which does not only apply to American citizens but also to prospective citizens, one of which I consider myself to be. As your telegram asks me to call on you any day of the week, I shall call next Wednesday October 23rd, unless you advise me to the contrary. I should be grateful if you could keep the contents of this letter secret as my mother, who is still living in Germany, might get into difficulties if it became known that I am willing to join an army the possibility of whose becoming a hostile force to Germany exists.[12]

Claus attended at the US Consulate for an interview, but found that there were going to be delays: 'of course their future action, if any, regarding the war was unpredictable. These uncertainties, and a sense of obligation to this country, motivated me to volunteer for the British forces immediately.' On 28 October 1940, Claus travelled to Oxford to volunteer for the British forces. He was signed up at the Army recruiting centre in New Inn Hall Street by Major Rowell and issued with a certificate:

> This is to certify that the bearer C.L.O. Ascher whose Alien Registration Certificate bears the number 675926 has this day applied to enlist into the Army, and that his application is under consideration.

That day, Claus took the Oath of Allegiance to King George VI and his descendants and received the King's shilling. This he did with great pride: 'Captain Napier who presided over Albright House, in his understanding and helpful way, approved with the words: "it will give you a country".' Claus was still not a British citizen. He was now numbered with around 4,000 other ex-Germans and ex-Austrians who were donning the British Army uniform that autumn. For the next two months, he patiently waited at Wallingford for further instructions about his enlistment into the army. Then in December 1940 he finally received instructions to report to Ilfracombe on the rugged, picturesque North Devon coast for training in the Pioneer Corps. He prepared to leave the farm training colony where he had been since his arrival in Britain nearly two years earlier. It had taught him much:

> It was an introduction for me to England. I was living with the average English fellow and some refugees. Those in charge served the welfare of the boys quite unselfishly. Friendliness and tolerance were rather new to me and in complete contrast to regimented Nazi Germany.

Claus was about to become one of 10,000 German and Austrian refugees who volunteered for the British forces throughout the course of the war. These men and women became affectionately known as the 'King's most loyal enemy aliens'.[13] Claus's loyalty was never in doubt:

> I was firmly on the side of Britain, about to join her forces to fight against Germany, the country of my birth. It was a momentous time and one of which I am immensely proud.

CHAPTER 4

The Pioneer Corps

On New Year's Eve 1940, Claus Ascher reported to the Pioneer Corps training centre at Ilfracombe. It was here that he underwent six weeks of basic army training. 'No one was terribly interested in a new recruit that day,' he comments. 'Someone gave me a blanket and showed me a room in an unoccupied house. Everyone got increasingly merrier and disinterested in me.' By now the seaside town had already seen hundreds of Continental recruits pass through for training during the autumn of 1940.[14] The men whom Claus trained with there were all ex-Germans and ex-Austrians who, like him, had been classified as 'enemy aliens' at the outbreak of war.

> Soon things fell into place and I was given a uniform. I was very proud of the brass buttons which I diligently polished all the time I had them. Being in British army uniform was enormously important because, although we were all German-speaking comrades, it was not yet a metamorphosis into being a British soldier, but it was *the* first step on the way to feeling British.

Claus was issued with his pay book and given army number 13805191, the first four digits denoting his status as an 'enemy alien' in the British forces. Gradually he was introduced to army practice. That winter of 1940–41 was a particularly memorable one because it was so harsh:

> It was a bitterly cold, freezing winter. The steep roads of Ilfracombe were very icy in early January 1941. We had been given new army boots with studs on

which were not particularly easy on the icy pavements. We were apt to sit down rather unceremoniously on our bottoms!

Claus found himself training alongside refugee men of all ages, some of whom were amongst the foremost intellectuals of German and Austrian society: doctors, lawyers, dentists, surgeons, engineers, mathematicians, artists and musicians. With so many Continental intellectuals training in the 'alien' Pioneer Corps, Ilfracombe was transformed into a microcosm of German and Austrian life. All had fled Nazi Germany and Austria as refugees from Nazi oppression. Some had arrived in Britain as early as 1933, but the majority, like Claus, came in 1939. Amongst the notables who passed through Ilfracombe for army training were Viennese lawyer Martin Freud, eldest son of Sigmund Freud,[15] journalist Arthur Koestler,[16] newspaper tycoon Robert Maxwell and artist Johannes Matthaeus Koelz. Lectures were held in the evenings, forming a small university. All subjects were covered in the arts, science, mathematics, economics and languages.

There was a pool of musical talent too. An orchestra had already been formed under the direction of Breslau-born violinist and conductor Max Strietzel who organised performances and shows with Coco the Clown (aka Nicolai Poliakoff). The shows were a huge success, usually hosted at Ilfracombe's garrison theatre for the local population. It boosted morale in wartime and raised funds for the war effort.[17] The Christmas of 1940 saw the production of *Cinderella*. The lead role of Prince Charming was played by Helen Poliakoff, one of Coco's daughters, and Cinderella by Jean Coles, the eldest daughter of Colonel Coles, the commanding officer of the training centre. Refugee prima ballerina Hanne Musch was Gita the Gipsy, with Jack Norman and Olaf Olsen as the ugly stepsisters. The impressive scenery and settings had been painted by refugee artist Private Gurschner. Music was provided by members of the continental army orchestra under Max Strietzel. That included: Cecil Aronowitz, G. Guttmann, Hans Geiger, H. Hirschfeld (no relation of Willy), S. Mark, H. Moses, W. Kornfeld, H. Adler, Fritz Lustig, H. Harpuder, H. Kruh, F. Taylor, M. Maschowski, A. Neustadt and W. Stiasny. Claus Ascher attended some of the shows during the short time that he was there:

> On one occasion during a variety show there was a demonstration of all sorts of exciting tricks. Volunteers were asked to go onto the stage with the promise of a beer drinking contest to see who could finish his pint most quickly. The reward was being allowed to dance with the showgirls afterwards. Ever eager to have a go, I nipped up onto the stage. We stayed in our seats on stage after during an act of electrical tricks by the performer in a smart Spanish style rig

who did wonderful things with electric bulbs and strip lights which appeared to light by themselves. Then he asked those of us seated on stage to hold short rods for him – only to discover that we could not let go of them once he had thrown a switch. The audience greatly enjoyed our contorted facial expressions. When he allowed us to let go, we were still seated in that row of chairs but not for long as he swept a rapier across the floor of the stage, sparks from studs in the seats of our chairs made us get up *very* quickly! But at least we did get to dance with the girls.

Of his time in the seaside town, he concludes: 'I enjoyed my short time in Ilfracombe. I was issued with a pickaxe handle with which to stand on guard. And that was my duty – to stand under the palm trees along the promenade. It made me feel awfully romantic: to be a British soldier standing on duty under the palms. Now any correspondence to my mother in Germany via my sister Suzanne in America had to avoid any hints of my having joined the British forces. Later, after America joined the war, contact was limited to very rare and unreliable attempts at sending twenty-five-word messages through the Red Cross.'

After training in Ilfracombe, Claus was assigned to 87 Company of the Pioneer Corps. The company had originally been raised in the early spring of 1940 in Kitchener Camp, a refugee transit camp near Sandwich in Kent.[18] In March that year, it landed in France and commenced work with the Royal Army Ordnance Corps at the port of Le Havre before moving to Harfleur. The following month they were joined by 88 Company and engaged in guarding the docks at Harfleur. With the fall of Dunkirk in May 1940 and the risk of a German invasion of Britain, 87 Company was evacuated from France with other troops in June 1940. On returning to England, 87 Company was sent to Bideford in North Devon to re-group. The men were transferred to Somerset engaged in defence work and bomb disposal. In January 1941, they transferred from there to Blackheath, south of the River Thames, clearing the bombed areas in Woolwich. It was here, a few weeks later, that Claus Ascher joined them. Now based in south London, Claus's main duties with other German refugees in 87 Company consisted of clearing bomb damage at the height of the Blitz on London. After a time the men were moved to billets in a slightly damaged, derelict house in Vanbrugh Terrace, Blackheath. It was at this time that Claus met a pretty girl called Sadie Bird at a dance and experienced his first kiss:

We stepped outside into the garden of the house where the dance had taken place. It took me ages to pluck up my courage and to plant a Chaste Salute on her cheek. It was bitterly cold and there was snow on the ground. Sadie was wearing flimsy dancing pumps and her feet must have been wet through and absolutely frozen, as was her cheek. This was the first time I had ever kissed a girl – I was just nineteen years old. In spite of my awkward and immature behaviour, she agreed to see me again and I would walk her home to Brockley. On the way there were two surface air raid shelters in which we would exchange kisses and I became more practised in that art! On one occasion, this could have got me into serious trouble because it was my turn to do fire-watching duty. And no sooner had we said goodbye that the sirens went. I ran all the way and just made it back to our billet in time before my absence from duty was noticed. In due course, Sadie stood me up at a date and dumped me. I can't say I can blame her. I must have been an awful, immature bore.

From Blackheath the men eventually travelled everyday to the Plumstead area, again to deal with bomb damage:

There was one particular site that was badly damaged and it was here that I learned something about the construction of pre-war buildings in London that I found rather shocking. Poor quality mortar had been used and the explosion had reduced it to sand such that the bricks were stacked on each other with sand in between. We separated and stacked the bricks as best we could, to tidy up the site. I learnt to walk alongside the damaged wall, swinging a sledgehammer to knock out every second brick. After I had done that, I gingerly lent against the wall and began pushing in a rhythm. On the third push, I would step aside and the wall would usually come tumbling down. The only really solid part was the chimneys which were the main support on which the whole house hung. Occasionally I came across a piece of properly constructed wall where the bricks were difficult to separate and where proper cement mortar had been used, presumably that was when the building inspector had come around and checked it. Most of the houses had bricks spaced for ventilation which were on strips of concrete laid on earth, about the width of a brick. I discovered that this was what the whole house was standing on. I did not have a very great respect for British pre-war development.

Our base was a bare bombsite on which we stacked our tools, had our bonfire and lunch and tea breaks. Soon we became acquainted with the local people. I remember with particular affection Dave King, a builder, who had a motorcycle and a sidecar in which he carried his stuff and transported his beautiful Alsatian dog. The dog became quite fond of us, especially as we fed him snacks. When Dave King came back from a job, he would whistle and the dog would leap into the sidecar and be taken home. The King family lived in a house overlooking the back of the cemetery. Mr and Mrs King invited me to stay with them when

I was granted a week's leave, in February or March 1941 in response to cinema appeals at the time to extend hospitality to soldiers. That is when I used to spend the nights with them in the air raid shelter and became acquainted with their friends and neighbours, as well as the ARP personnel whom we joined to do such rescue work as we could. Doing this work and living in the shelters every night, I got to know the south-east Londoners and developed a great respect for these people who did not pretend to be better than anyone else. In their calm and coolest way, they took events as they came. These were tough times; no one knew from day to day whose house would be the next to be struck by a bombing raid. The local people knew about my German background. All of us in 87 Company were soldiers with German accents, but still they were very kind to us. They knew why we had come to England and held no resentment against us for the daily blitz by the Luftwaffe. After all we were still German, but we experienced no hostility. They didn't like Hitler but they appreciated that we were on their side, not with the Germans even though that had been the country of our birth.

I also joined the parties which went out to rescue people from the rubble once a landmine had hit.

Bombs inflicted structural damage, especially to the flimsy types of houses in the area, but landmines were large blast bombs floating down on parachutes to ensure they exploded on the surface and did maximum damage to buildings. They could flatten a whole block of houses and that was where we pulled people out of the rubble, many still alive looking like red Indians from being covered in brick dust. I also remember the noise of clusters of shrapnel from our own anti-aircraft barrage coming down, sounding like a swarm of bees. Once when I was standing beside an ARP Warden, there was a sudden ding-dong sound like a bell and both our helmets were suddenly at an acute angle in opposite directions, apparently struck by a piece of shrapnel glancing from the rim of one helmet to the other. It was a demonstration and reminder of the usefulness of the steel helmet! This was the period when I got to know, like, and admire these splendid people, their cool courage and indomitable sense of humour!

On 16 March 1941, 87 Company moved from south London to Bootle near Liverpool. The men were originally destined for Wales but instead were diverted for a time to Liverpool where a group of conscientious objectors were engaged in fire watching duties on the rooftops of the tall Victorian warehouses. 'It was slightly uncomfortable standing on top of the roofs with the thought of what happens when the bombers start coming, but fortunately we just missed the blitz on the city.' The heavy raids on Liverpool started just after they left and so they were lucky in that respect. During their time there, they were billeted in unoccupied houses in the Sefton Park area of Liverpool:

> One of my friends in 87 Company at this time was Eugene Reimann, of Latvian origin. He was known to us by the Russian affectionate diminutive of that name, 'Zhenia' or 'Jenia'. He was a larger than life character, physically very energetic and lively. Before he joined the Pioneer Corps he had been in censorship and billeted with a family in Liverpool who had a daughter of our age. It was from the censorship job that he joined the Pioneer Corps. He was an enthusiastic communist and in favour of the Soviet occupation of the Baltic countries at that time. He had once been in the cavalry and regaled us with stories of his time there. He had several girlfriends at any one time whilst we were in Liverpool, but one in particular fell deeply in love with him. She was Pat Cleland, the daughter of the people he was billeted with. Sometime later when we were writing letters from our barrack rooms in Wales, he suddenly looked disturbed and said: 'did I put the letter addressed to Pam into the envelope addressed to Pat?' Eugene eventually introduced me to the Cleland family. It was they who took me under their wing and were very good to me. On army leave later on, I always spent some time with the Clelands in Liverpool. The parents were like a father and mother to me. Their daughter Pat had become an enthusiastic communist due to her affection for Eugene. Pat and I often had political arguments in a comradely sort of way. I was not in favour of any extreme politics, whether left-wing or right-wing. Eugene was eventually accepted for some kind of special service, but was tragically killed when he rode a motorbike too enthusiastically during training, as was his style. Pat never forgot him and never got over it. She never married. The Clelands remained my life long friends and were to become my adopted family later whilst I was in the commandos.

Thousands of pioneer soldiers like Claus were desperate to transfer to other units or regiments. They became increasingly frustrated at talent wasted in a labour corps. This was *their* war. They wanted to fight and have an active part in the downfall of Hitler and the Nazis. In the first two years of their army service, this was denied them because the Pioneer Corps remained the only unit open to the 'enemy aliens'.

All this changed in 1942. At the beginning of that year, the British government realised the potential of the German-speaking refugees for special operations because of their fluency in the German language. Transfers from the Pioneer Corps were at this stage only for 'special missions'; others would have to wait until 1943 to serve in combat regiments of the British forces. During 1942, those head-hunted for special missions would undergo training for three new top-secret units: the Small Scale Raiding Force (SSRF), Commandos and Special Operations Executive (SOE).[19] The first group to be formed for hazardous missions was the SSRF, a kind of early commando unit. They received specialised top-secret training at Anderson Manor near Blandford in Dorset. From there, small groups of five or six men, usually with one German speaker, were sent on coastal raids into North Africa, Norway and Normandy. The aim of their missions was to test enemy defences, take German POWs for interrogation and to gather intelligence. As well as them, a group of German-speaking refugees were about to also undergo intensive training to be an elite group of commandos.

Already, in 1941, a mysterious older gentleman by the name of Hartmann, who spoke German with a distinct Swiss intonation, began to move amongst soldiers of 87 and 88 Pioneer companies. It was whilst 87 Company was stationed in Liverpool that Hartmann lived for a time in the billets asking numerous questions about their motivation and attitude. Some of those of Austrian background suddenly disappeared and did not return. It later turned out that they were accepted for Special Operations Executive, as in the case of Anton Walter Freud (grandson of Sigmund Freud), who was also in 87 Company.[20] Hartmann's path crossed that of Claus. Little did Claus know then that the course of his war was to change. He was subjected to various questioning by Hartmann, but as he says: 'We were used to not asking too many questions. There was a war on.' He continues:

We were puzzled as to what an elderly man with a strong Swiss accent was doing in a Pioneer company full of central European refugees. A private of a Pioneer Corps unit amongst us privates? It was very odd. He never talked about his background and much to our amusement his favourite adjective was 'fan-DASS-disch' (fantastic). He probed the attitude, orientation and motivations of those of us who had applied for transfer to fighting units. It was always individually, never whilst we were with any of our colleagues. He tended to pick us out individually and conduct a conversation. He once mused whether it would be a good idea if people like us who spoke fluent German could have special training and be dropped by parachute behind enemy lines. He asked our view on whether it would be a good idea if the Germans could be distracted from what was going on by simultaneously having an air raid around us. We could be dropped in the middle of the mayhem and noise. I replied that I did not think it was a very good idea and that I would much rather be dropped quietly rather than attract enemy attention with air activity. By probing our views, Hartmann started to build a view of us. We learnt much later that he was actually a Colonel in Intelligence.

On 29 April 1941, 87 Company was on the move again. The men were transferred from Liverpool to Velindre in South Wales where they were billeted in an old woollen mill. Duties consisted of laying pipelines, minefields and barbed wire obstacle defences along the coast. By 1 July, three sections of the company were still laying minefields, five sections were engaged on camp defence work and one was working at a coal dump. It was a memorable summer:

> The summer of 1941 was a gorgeous one. In the beautiful wooded hills of that area it was idyllic, but there was another angle to this idyll for me. Whilst the company was first on parade in the mornings and then taken to beaches to lay mines and wire defences, I became a member of the newly formed band and orchestra. The members of the orchestra, including myself were relieved of Pioneer duties. My best friend in our section of 87 company was Karl Walter Billmann. He had come to England from Munich where he had been a music student and studied conducting. He was a very good oboist and had brought his oboe with him.

One of the officers was Lieutenant Henry Wood. He decided to emulate his famous namesake and start an orchestra and band. As already mentioned, there was a fair amount of musical talent in the Pioneer Corps companies, as to be expected with German and Austrian intellectuals. Lt Wood obtained instruments wherever he could and established an orchestra and dance band. The purpose was to travel around and give concerts.

> We did our best, even if it wasn't wonderful. My friend Karl was the sub-conductor and assigned to training the orchestra. He was part of the dance band too, headed by a fabulous musician called Frankie Baron who was an absolutely perfect pianist. In all the time I knew him, I never once heard him make a mistake on the piano. When he sat down to play classical music, he was as perfect as when he played dance music.

One day Claus was in a pub enjoying a glass of beer when Lt Henry Wood saw him and said: 'Ascher, you recently borrowed a cello from the orchestra because you played cello in Germany, didn't you?' But what Lt Wood could not know was that Claus could no longer play properly. He said: 'We need a double bass player, report to the band hut tomorrow morning.' And that is how Claus became a member of both the orchestra and dance band: 'It made life idyllic because we were excused the working parades because we tended to travel all over the country in open trucks with our instruments. We returned to base very late, so we were excused morning parades and normal pioneer duties because we had to practice in the daytime. We also played music for our own benefit, particularly chamber music. I was involved in Schubert's *Trout Quintet* which has a bass part. We really enjoyed ourselves. I took the opportunity of dancing whenever I could.' He became particularly fond of a local lady friend who helped to accentuate that idyllic summer of 1941. That girlfriend was Beryl Griffiths from Swansea who was staying with her aunt at Trefach, Velindre:

> She was a very nice, attractive, natural girl whom I met at a dance at which we played. We became girlfriend and boyfriend. She was lively and good company, and we became fond of each other. For me, she was the spirit of that golden summer. In due course, we were parted by the circumstances of wartime and military postings as experienced by so many people at that time. There was no real heartbreak over her but I do remember her with affection.

On 13 August 1941 the company moved to Tenby. Here too Claus remained in the band and orchestra, which held dances in the local ballroom of the town. The location offered the opportunity for a good deal of swimming. Whilst Claus continued to be excused normal pioneer duties with other members of the orchestra, fellow soldiers were engaged on hutting and camp defence work; wiring, laying pipeline or general training. This was to change less than two months later when, on 2 October 1941, the men were transferred to the Defensible Barracks at Pembroke Dock. The Defensible Barracks was a large Victorian fortification, still with its original moat although no longer full of water. The former drawbridge, now fixed, was also a memorable feature. It was an odd feeling:

> There I stood, a German in British Army uniform, on sentry duty at the barrack gates overlooking Milford Haven. It was a bizarre situation.

Inside the complex there were old-style barracks, consisting of a large open square which served as the parade ground, surrounded by buildings. The fortification still had battlements with gun platforms which were for Spigot guns, having a pillar in the middle of a circular disc base of slate on which the points of the compass were engraved:

> The Spigot gun was essentially a gun barrel with a vertical seating bore by which it can be mounted on a spigot on top of the pillar and swivelled to point in any direction and from which it can be lifted off or back on as required. We never saw any of the archaic guns which had commanded the Milford Haven, only the old mounting pillars were left.

The pioneer soldiers were not the only personnel stationed at the Defensible Barracks. There were also WAAFs (Women's Auxiliary Air Force) working in shifts in the basement. The men naturally became friendly with them; Claus with Jean who did not talk about her work because the women were all bound by the Official Secrets Act, but: 'I began to gather that they had radio sets. They were effectively one of the listening posts, probably linked to Bletchley Park. It was thanks to my friendship with Jean that I became an associate member of the YWCA at Pembroke Dock which was frequented by the WAAFs. It was the only service club catering for service personnel in that run-down, partly derelict town and granted associate membership to several members of 87 Company.'

The men of 87 Company had some weapons training whilst in the Pioneer Corps but not until they arrived at the Defensible Barracks. They were issued with Canadian Ross rifles, but there were only enough for half the company so they took turns to stand sentry duty with the weapons. It was from the Defensible Barracks that the men fanned out to different locations to carry out work in the surrounding areas. Mine-laying was a major part of the duties. Band activity had now ceased and Claus was engaged in regular Pioneer duties:

> With my section of 87 Company, I was involved in digging out a reservoir somewhere along the Milford Haven area in Pembrokeshire. We worked hard, digging with pneumatic drills. But I found in the slate of the rock, a pneumatic drill was not necessarily the best instrument because it would get stuck in the strata of the slate. My favourite instrument was the heavy crowbar. If it could be aimed properly, it was possible to split off the various layers quite easily and I became something of a crowbar expert. It was at this time that my girlfriend Jean started to date a Czech member of our company and I took much of my emotional reaction out on the Welsh slate!

In the late spring of 1942, disaster struck at the Defensible Barracks. It happened during a lecture on mines, in connection with the men's mine-laying work. On 28 April 1942 Major Geoffrey Garratt, who had been posted to the Pioneer Corps because he was an active communist, was giving a demonstration for Pioneer soldiers and a party of Royal Engineers using live explosives. It ended in disaster when two mines exploded, killing Major Garratt and several men. 'For days afterwards, we had to scrape bits of dead body off the walls.' A fellow member of Claus's company wrote about this incident in his memoirs. Garry Rogers (born Günther Baumgart) served first in 87 Company and then, in 1943, transferred to the First Royal Tank Regiment. He wrote in *Interesting Times*:

We were now issued with Lee Enfield rifles and received training in the use of weapons. One such training session led to a disaster. The cause was never discovered, but during a training lecture on grenades, a live grenade exploded and caused a major accident in which five soldiers were killed and a number badly injured. The force of the explosion was so severe that it blew out windows and even damaged thick walls. One soldier was blown clear out of the window and into the moat.[21]

That day seventeen men died, two of whom were 'alien' Pioneers. They were Corporal Heinz Abraham aged twenty-three (13801220) and Private Heinz Schwartze aged twenty-two (13801014). The others who died were British-born soldiers from the Pioneer Corps, Royal Engineers and King's Own Scottish Borderers. All are buried in the Pembroke Dock Military Cemetery which is maintained by the Commonwealth War Graves Commission.[22]

During the summer of 1942 Claus was sent on a special weaponry course which he attended with Anton Walter Freud:[23] 'Walter and I were in different sections of 87 Company, and never had any contact until we were both part of a group of volunteers who attended a course of field craft and weapons training in a tented camp in South Wales, lasting for about two weeks.' Afterwards they returned to their respective Pioneer sections, with many Pioneers engaged on the large-scale construction of Nissen huts in preparation for the arrival of American troops in Britain. America had reluctantly joined the war after the Japanese bombing of Pearl Harbor in the Pacific Ocean the previous December. Thousands of American troops had to be accommodated in army camps across Britain. Many of the 'alien' Pioneer companies, including 87 Company, were given the task of constructing these camps during 1942.

A short time later, during the summer of 1942, Claus, his friend Karl Walter Billmann and other volunteers from 87 Company, received a rail warrant to travel to London to report at the Grand Central Hotel in Marylebone Road. It was here that they were to be interviewed for possible acceptance into the 'special forces'. The hotel served as a transit hub. 'It was an exciting and mysterious place. At last something was happening for us.'

It was full of people carrying tropical kit, disappearing around the corners of corridors. Each morning we had to study the notice board to see whether there was anything about ourselves. If there was not, we would go off down the Marylebone Road as far as Baker Street, turn right, and on the left hand side there was a café called The Bakers Oven. We treated ourselves to a pot of tea and toast with marmalade. Then it was back to the Grand Central Hotel where we were staying. It was all very exciting, until one day our names were on the notice board to report for our interviews.

Claus was required to report to a specific room at 10 a.m. and found himself in front of civilians who were to interview and vet him. There were also military officers and a medical officer present. As the week progressed, at the end of this process, the ranks of interviewees thinned out and were sent back to their units. Those who were still there were informed that one of the interviewing officers wished to see them. It was Captain Brian Hilton-Jones who was to form a troop of commandos. During the interview, Captain Hilton-Jones made a point of stressing that they were not a spying organisation or anything of that sort. In Hilton-Jones's words, they were 'a perfectly straightforward military unit'. Once the vetting process had been completed at the Grand Central Hotel, Claus was informed by Hilton-Jones that he had been accepted for commando service. He would become a member of a troop under the command of Hilton-Jones. Claus was extremely proud to have been accepted. 'At that point,' he says, 'we knew that we had been accepted for something special.'

The men who had passed the interview stage were then sent off on leave, to report at the end of it to the Pioneer Corps depot in Yorkshire. They collected their pay, warrants and passes. During the period of leave, Claus travelled to Liverpool to visit the Clelands family. He also requested a railway warrant to Edinburgh, from where the same warrant would allow him to return to Pembroke Dock via Liverpool where he could break the journey. The men had to get back to their unit to pick up their kit before reporting to Bradford. In Edinburgh Claus visited a family he had known in Bad Homburg. After the period of leave, Claus and the other men who had been accepted into the commandos reported to the Pioneer Corps depot in Bradford. They waited for the next stage:

> But we were not awfully well behaved because we were on an emotional high having just been accepted for the special forces. We were billeted in a bomb damaged mews of garages which was full of two-tier bunks. The houses facing the main road were also rather damaged. If we did not feel like going through the gate and booking ourselves in and out, we had an alternative plan. There was a trapdoor in the ceiling of our garage room, which was easily accessible from the top bunk. It led through a bomb damaged house straight onto the main road. A group of our men who couldn't be bothered to sneak in via the bombed property, but brazenly walked through the gate in spite of having been out after hours, were challenged by an inexperienced young Pioneer Corps soldier who asked: 'halt, who goes there?' And they replied, 'Friend, advance

to be recognised'. The inexperienced soldier then approached and the men would say to him: 'yes, very good. Well done, my man. Carry on.' And then they proceeded to walk straight through the gate unchallenged.

On other occasions there was an inspection towards bedtime to see whether we were all there because we had not behaved in a very disciplined manner. We were aware that we were no longer under their discipline and I'm afraid it was more or less up to us whether we reported for duty or not, or attended the parade. The soldiers would march off to do some Pioneer Corps duties somewhere. Every time the marching column turned a corner, the tail dropped off and we went off to see our girlfriends in the area. There was one occasion, an inspection was held to make sure everyone was in. Some of us distracted the inspecting officer whilst the trapdoor would open and those of us who were missing would drop onto the bunks. Presently we were banished to a mill on the moors under a strict disciplinarian Sgt. Major. He suffered dreadfully because we were not strictly under his control and played him up something horrible. We had an unfair advantage over him. We led a merry life – part of which was girlfriends. But that social life with girlfriends soon ended when we were transferred to the mill on the Yorkshire Moors.

It was at this mill on the Yorkshire moors that Captain Hilton-Jones appeared with a stack of new army pay books. The men were to be given new army numbers and a parent regiment which would disguise their real operations in the commandos. The first instruction Hilton-Jones gave the men was to change their German names to something more English. The new name would be entered in the pay books and was for their own protection because serving abroad, especially in raids behind the lines, if they were captured they would be treated as traitors and not POWs:

Hilton-Jones called us in one by one and asked us for our new names and also details of reliable British friends who could act as our next-of-kin and main contact. He advised us that it had been decided by Army Council Order that we should change our names for the sake of security, and that we should appoint reliable British friends as our 'next-of-kin' contacts, rather than some alternative like isolating us in some secret camp and pretending we had all disappeared. This, he said, 'would have reeked of mystery' and attracted unwelcome curiosity. Volunteers from all units and services were *attached* to their commandos, but remained on the strength of their 'parent units' who paid them, and whose cap badges they wore in their green berets. They retained their designation as rifleman, gunner or fusilier. They reverted to their parent units when the Commandos were disbanded at the end of the war, unlike the marines who *belonged* to the Royal Marine Commandos rather than being attached to them. This was why we were allocated to 'Parent Units' (in my case the Royal Sussex Regt.) It was part and parcel of the name change. An English name from the Pioneer Corps with the alien prefix number 1380 would have been incongruous.

Our new names were entered in our pay books and the new next-of- kin who were the only ones who knew both our names. Friends and acquaintances from our old life who know us under our old names should not know our new names for security reasons. The Clelands became my next-of-kin. Much to her disgust, Pat Cleland was entered in my pay book as my aunt. By a strange coincidence, the Clelands had a senior civil servant billeted on them whom I also got to know during subsequent visits to Liverpool. He was a very pleasant, dapper, quiet and courteous gentleman named Dawkins, member of a War Office department which had been evacuated from London on account of the bombing. For some reason Pat nicknamed him 'Blossom'. It was not until after the war that we learned that he had been the head of a casualty section, and the *only* person who had in his safe a list of the original and new, anglicised names of the members of 3 Troop, side-by-side! And that, when I was wounded, he had known long before the Clelands, in their capacity of next-of-kin, had been informed.

I had to think of a new name which was not so straightforward because all the obvious surnames beginning with A had already been taken by my comrades: Andrews, Anderson. We knew it was wise to keep our original initials in case we began writing our old names having forgotten out new names, but could easily switch to our new ones. Just at that moment, an Anson twin engine communications aircraft flew over, so that became the inspiration for my name. I became Colin Anson. It is very English and not common. Hilton-Jones then looked up and said: 'no middle name? It is customary.' Out of thin air, I chose Edward. And that is how Claus Leopold Octavio Ascher became Colin Edward Anson.

Not only were their names changed, but the men had to fashion a new family history to mask their origins. For those who were later captured and interrogated as POWs it meant creating a cover story along the lines of having had a German education because their father was a businessman who had travelled and worked abroad. Protecting their real identity as Germans or Austrians was paramount. An elaborate system was worked out for sending and receiving post:

Our new next-of-kin, in my case the Clelands, would liaise with our relatives and friends from our former lives. They acted as necessary intermediaries for our post and letters. Friends would write to us under our old name and the trusted family would then put it in another envelope with our new name on it. That security never broke down.

Soon after the change of name, the men received their marching orders. Colin Anson, as he now was, and his comrades were about to start one of the most exciting periods of their lives in which their physical fitness would be tested to the limit. Colin was to be part of some of the fittest, elite men of His Majesty's forces and still as a German national.

CHAPTER 5

Commando Training

I n 1942 Prime Minister Winston Churchill sanctioned the formation of No.10 Inter-Allied Commando. As part of that, Lord Louis Mountbatten suggested the creation of a German-speaking unit called 3 Troop after he became Chief of Combined Operations that same year. The purpose was to train specialist fighters to carry out clandestine intelligence operations and raids, and where necessary be attached to other regiments for secret missions. A number of commando units were raised during the progress of the war but only 3 Troop, also known as X Troop, consisted solely of German-speaking refugees. That included Colin. Just over a hundred German-speaking refugees trained as part of 3 Troop of No.10 Inter-Allied Commando under the command of Captain Brian Hilton-Jones, affectionately known as 'the Skipper' or 'Hilly'. The troop constituted different nationalities, primarily Germans and Austrians but also Hungarians and Czechs. It was an unlikely coalition but all were united by the fact that they spoke fluent German and had a common cause – to fight the evil regime that had ruined their lives and continued to threaten their families who were left behind in Nazi-occupied Europe. They had a central role to play because they were the only commando troop that did not go into action together. They were detached from 3 Troop in twos or threes and attached to other commando units for special duties which included the use of the German language. Their leader, Captain Hilton-Jones, had originally served with 4 Commando and taken part in the Dieppe Raid. One of Colin's comrades of 3 Troop, Ian Harris, (originally

Hans Hajos) described Hilton-Jones as 'a tough, wiry guy who could speak German and had been a junior official in the British Embassy in Berlin. He was a great example. He turned most of us into something quite formidable.' Colin's parent regiment was the Royal Sussex Regiment, new army number 6436355. This was to mask the fact of having been in the Pioneer Corps which would have given away their German origin.

The men left the mill on the Yorkshire moors and set out by train for their new base whilst in Britain. They headed for Aberdovey in West Wales. Colin comments:

> It was across country on the train that we changed our Pioneer Corps cap badges for those of the parent units to which we had been allocated. We also started using our new names and arrived in Aberdovey, not as regular soldiers but as commando recruits. The policemen in Abeydovey had been advised of the real nature of things and that there was a group of soldiers with German accents in the area. The rest of the population probably caught on fairly rapidly, but was very tactful and security conscious. We were not there very long, just enough to be allocated billets in private houses. One of the privileges given to us was that we were no longer treated like soldiers who lived in barrack rooms, marching from noon to night. Instead we were paid a subsistence allowance of 6s 8d a day, from which we paid for our billets. We were allowed to change accommodation if we wished. We were treated almost as civilian employees. We were trusted to be responsible and to report for parades as and when ordered. The rest of the time we could do as we pleased. Myself, my friends Karl Walter Billman who was now Ken Bartlett, with David Stewart (Strauss) and Robbie Villiers (Fogel) had billets with Mr and Mrs Edwards in Church Street, Aberdovey. Later, their daughter became a good friend to me and my wife Alice.

Over the course of a year the men would receive the most intensive and gruelling training that the British army could offer, consisting of eight-mile jog-marches before breakfast, rock climbing, abseiling down sheer cliffs above rough seas, parachuting, mountaineering in Snowdonia, boating training on the South Coast and armed and unarmed combat. Only live ammunition was used during exercises. It was very demanding, intended to weed out those whose heart was not in it. Colin's colleague Ian Harris recalls:

> We had equipment that no one else had. The purpose of our training was to train us as individual fighters rather than part of a unit. We were the first to be issued with the Dennison smock, later universally accepted as the uniform for parachutists; a camouflage jacket and Green Beret, boots with special grip,

a Tommy Gun and a Colt pistol. We were given Shetland wool pullovers and special wearing apparel. I wrote to my parents: 'they are treating us like gentlemen here.' We were given double meat rations, private billets and not in Nissen huts.

In October 1942 the men were sent for their first period of basic commando training at Achnacarry between Loch Arkaig and the Great Glen in the Highlands of Scotland. They arrived by train at the nearest station at Spean Bridge. From there they had to march at hell a of a pace to Achnacarry House:

We were met on the station platform by Viscount de Jonghe from the Belgian Troop. He was a tall man with very long legs. He wasn't carrying anything, so he marched us off at a tremendous pace. He was known thereafter as the 'nimble-footed viscount'. With all our kit, we struggled to keep up with him. This was our first introduction to the physical demands of our training and what lay ahead for us.

The men were marched from Spean Bridge station to where the road crosses the Caledonian Canal via a lock gate. Then having crossed it in a northerly direction, they turned right along the loch until it veered in land slightly towards Achnacarry House. They were to return by the same route at the end of the course. It was at Achnacarry that the men underwent over two weeks of incredibly demanding training designed to test them to the limit. Colin recalls how tough it was:

We did all manner of things which we would not normally consider ourselves capable of doing. It was a very cleverly designed course, and step by step things got increasingly more difficult. We were given challenges which we would not have dared in the very beginning. There was a great emphasis on physical fitness and so most of the time we were totally exhausted. Sometimes we were so tired we marched in our sleep and then realised we actually *were* marching for real because we bumped into the man in front of us. There was also an insistence on smartness which was not easy after we had been crawling through the mud during our exercises. Everything had to be polished and clean so that by the end of the day we were ready for a good turn-out the following morning. I recall that often we had sleepy-eyed sessions under the swinging bulb in stables. We did a good deal of running and marching, but also a certain amount of field craft, rock climbing and abseiling. We did not have the specialist equipment which the army uses today. We simply had our toggle ropes, a fairly short length of rope with a wooden toggle at one end and loop at the other. It was possible to put the toggle ropes together if needed threading the toggle of one through the loop of another. We learnt how to build a toggle bridge which consisted of one elevated rope to walk on, two to act as railings and connecting ropes between the upper and lower ones.

Colin and his comrades also learnt how to master the dramatically termed 'death ride' which was a very quick way of crossing an obstacle without presenting themselves too much as a target for the enemy. The idea was that in action they might be faced with swimming or wading through a torrent or river to get over the other side. With a rope to anchor to a tree near the ground, the other end of the rope was taken up a tree as high as possible and tied to its trunk. They would climb up, having dampened their toggle rope beforehand, then put the toggle of their rope through its own loop to form a perfect circle. This would be thrown over the guide rope, and their hands placed through it either side, then they could kick off and zoom over the raging torrent: 'In our case, the practice runs were over a raging torrent from Loch Arkaig to Loch Lochy. We were able to zoom down the guide rope to the ground at the other end. It was quick and didn't expose us for too long as a target. My good friend and comrade David Stewart nearly came to grief on this death ride because he meticulously put his wrists through the rope, firmly grasped it and was about to kick off before he realised that he hadn't put the rope over the guide rope. He would have come straight down and drowned in the torrent. But he fortunately didn't. Commandos in other units were not so lucky and there were accidents on the "death ride" during training.'

Colin encountered some dangerous moments in training:

Abseiling is a normal rock climbing technique, not especially dangerous, but needed to be learnt. We did not have the harness and pulley equipment now commonly used for this technique. We found it advisable to stuff our leather jerkins under our behinds to prevent the friction from the rope singeing them! We trained on one particular tall rock which was simply a matter of stepping across a rope which had been fixed at the top on the flat. We were required to pick up the rope from behind us with our left hand, pull it over our left shoulder and pick up the bit of rope in front of us with our right hand, then walk backwards over the precipice and start to slide down, controlling one's descent by means of constricting the speed at which the rope would slip through one's left hand. We guided ourselves with our right hand, using the rope in front of us. I got it slightly wrong and suddenly found myself upside down. I remember Captain Hilton-Jones's face appearing over the precipice looking very concerned. 'Are you alright?' he said. 'Yes, sir, fine,' I replied. It happened too quickly to be frightened, but it could have easily ended in tragedy. I righted myself; that's how I learnt how to abseil.

Another vital part of training was in field craft, which was taught by demonstrators from Lord Lovat's special commando unit. The men had to learn to become 'invisible' if they were to operate behind enemy lines. Colin vividly remembers one such exercise which surprised them:

> One bright sunny morning we were arrayed on a hillside which sloped down to a shallow valley and rose again opposite us with a grass meadow. We were asked whether we could see anything. We said, 'Yes, there is a little red flag stuck in the middle of the field.'
>
> The instructor replied, 'Yes, but can you see anything else? Can you see anybody?'
>
> 'No,' we replied. 'There can't be anybody because there is no cover over there.'
>
> The officer then blew a whistle and suddenly the flag had gone. He blew another whistle and a dozen or more men stood up in the middle of the field which we had seen perfectly clearly. That was our first demonstration on how by using field craft, with scant cover, you can make yourself invisible and that was something we practiced a lot. In other exercises we had to learn to approach somewhere, or get away from a location, unseen. Our Sergeant Major O'Neill was one of the continentals in the commandos with a German accent. He would ring the doorbell of a house locally and ask the woman, 'have you seen anyone in your house, your garden?'
>
> 'No' she would reply. Then O'Neill would blow a whistle and up would stand half a dozen men. It gave us confidence to know that we could do that kind of thing.

There was much to learn in a relatively short space of time. The pace and level was always intense. Whilst at Achnacarry the men underwent other rigorous and dangerous exercises, some of which were opposed landings carried out on the 'Me-and-My-Pal' assault course. It was approached by paddling across a loch to perform an opposed landing. One of the key exercises for any commando unit for action in wartime was learning how to land on coastal areas of enemy territory. During these training exercises, the instructors at Achnacarry acted as the enemy and used live ammunition. 'They were extremely good shots,' comments Colin, 'and had their Bren guns on tripods. They took us under real fire so that we were used to being shot at whilst approaching the shore.' This was no game. The men had to be prepared for every eventuality. The instructors tested them to the limit in conditions as close to real warfare as possible:

> It was our instructors' great pride to fire bullet holes into the paddles of the folding boats which we were using to land. The boats were rather clumsy and heavy, of a loose wooden framework, connected to itself by canvas shape so

they could be collapsed and transported. We were in the boat on our knees, each with a short paddle, paddling like fury to get to our destination as quickly as possible whilst the bullets were crackling around us. We quickly got used to the sound of being shot at. Our aim was to approach the shore, get off as quickly as possible and spread out. Another exercise at Achnacarry involved the 'cat crawl' where we crossed an obstacle over a raging torrent by lying on top of the rope, one foot hooked over the rope, the other leg dangling down as far as you could, to provide a balancing counter-weight. We crawled like a cat across with the fast river underneath us. The one mistake to avoid was our weapon or pack suddenly swinging out sideways, because then we would find ourselves underneath the rope.

One of the assault courses was designed to practice the 'Me-and-My-Pal' technique in which one person advances while his pal covers him with fire from behind cover. And as soon as some good cover was found, that man went down behind it and start firing as the signal for his pal to start advancing, passing the lead man and so on. The men learnt how to advance close enough to the walls of a building for cover so as not to be shot at from the window. None of the exercises were without their risks as Colin remembers:

Once we were up tight against the wall of a house, we had to go through the motions of breaking the glass window with the butt of our weapon, then throwing a grenade in and storming the house itself. There was one casualty where one of the men who was simulating the smashing of the window pane had his thumb inside the trigger-guard and shot himself, but fortunately not fatally. It was a strenuous exercise, very instructive and we learnt a great deal from it. We were not the only trainees at Achnacarry. There were police, the only unit allowed to join commando training from 'civilian life'. They were used to serving in a hierarchical, uniformed organisation and to the level of discipline. All other recruits had to have served in the army first before joining a commando unit because there was not sufficient time in wartime to train them in basics. There were other troops of differing nationalities training at this time. One day whilst we were polishing our boots someone from another troop asked us: 'What lot are you? You're not British, are you?' One of my mates came out with the immortal words: 'You vill laugh, ve are British!'

The final exercise at Achnacarry was carried out over two days in November 1942 on half rations in freezing conditions. It was the most challenging assignment yet for Colin and his comrades in which they would get very wet and cold. The men were required to row across the loch in large rowing boats, with several sets of oars, to an opposed landing from different units. They had to achieve various tasks which included surviving a battle:

We rowed across the loch, aimed at the bottom of the cliff face which would give us cover, getting close to the shore. We had to avoid the obvious places to land which would be heavily defended, so instead approached under cover of a steep rock face. We had to jump into the water and got wet through before the scheme properly started. We then had to fight battles to proceed onwards from there. During that night, I stood on sentry duty to guard our resting place in a small wood. It was bright moonlight night, but I had to stay in the shadow and keep very still. Once you move, you become visible. When I did finally start moving a little, there was a curious crackling sound and it took me a moment to realise that it was my uniform which had been frozen solid. The ice broke as I moved. Then our skipper, Hilton-Jones, had a wonderful idea – we would light a fire in the woods as a decoy and then we retire to a nearby little wood and watch until the 'enemy' came. Then we could ambush them. A staff officer suddenly appeared, and proceeded to lecture Captain Hilton-Jones for lighting a fire and declared: 'You are all dead'. Hilton-Jones tried to explain that this was an ambush and we were waiting for the enemy. The staff officer would have none of it. Hilton-Jones swore and said to us, 'Bugger the scheme and the Colonel. I'm going to have breakfast'. Instead of putting out the fire, we used it to cook our half rations of bacon. We had nothing to worry about because we had all been declared dead anyway. One of our member suggested using one mess tin so as not to waste the fat from the bacon. We could then fry our piece of bread in it. I gave him my half ration but when I came back, he apologised – he had forgotten about the half ration and had eaten the lot!

After this final exercise, the men were officially passed out. 'We were,' says Colin, 'continuously kept at peak performance and fitness. We were now issued with our new green berets which we wore with great pride.' Achnacarry had tested and evaluated the new recruits, putting them through set-training routines of which there were not opportunities elsewhere. It was designed to establish that the men were physically capable of the commandos:

We had to prove a certain amount of physical and mental stamina, to show we would not hesitate in a given situation. For example, one obstacle course consisted of ramps made of horizontal tree trunks, fixed at intervals through a sloping angle, much like a crude ladder. As you approached it loaded down with your pack, ammunition and weapon, you had to maintain a certain pace to get up the high ramp. It was paramount that you did not hesitate or stop halfway because then you would not make it to the top and would fail the exercise. The point of the training was to get us to a certain standard *and* beyond, to push us to our limit. And if we could do that, we were up to the Commando missions. It also meant we were ready to move on to the next, more specialist, stage of our training, conducted by Captain Brian Hilton-Jones at Aberdovey.

Colonel Vaughan, who was in charge of the commando training depot at Achnacarry, had made no secret of the fact that he disliked the 'foreigners' of 3 Troop. Captain Hilton-Jones had had a hard time proving to him that they were worth their steel. Colin comments:

I even suspect it may have been made deliberately a bit harder for us to weed out anyone whose heart was not quite in it. Hilton-Jones instigated a form of special salute to impress Colonel Vaughan. On the command of 'eyes left', we would all stamp our left foot just once almost like a goose-step. We enjoyed doing that!

The men had one last farewell gesture for Colonel Vaughan. They marched off from Achnacarry training depot to Spean Bridge, significantly fitter men than when they had arrived. Colin recalls that day with some amusement:

We boarded our train and Colonel Vaughan was on the platform. We still had quite a number of thunder flashes left from the exercise. As the train pulled out, the platform rang out with the thunder flashes aimed at the feet of Colonel Vaughan. I shall never forget his look of surprise. I like to think he didn't forget us in a hurry.

It was at the change of trains at Glasgow with a substantial wait of two and a half hours before the connection was due to leave, and having been on half rations for the previous two days, that the men were ravenous. Captain Hilton-Jones suggested that they might like to leave the platform and find a nearby café. Colin and a group of mates found a respectable looking restaurant opposite the station and piled in:

We looked somewhat scruffy and adventurous and did not yet have our green berets – that came later in the journey. We were a bit boisterous and in no time cleared the cake stand. Then we each ordered a meal and more afterwards. By the time we had to leave for our train, we had really stuffed ourselves. We went over to the waitress to pay our bills, but she answered: 'No, the gentleman over there has paid for everything'. That was a pleasant unexpected surprise. We thanked the gentleman warmly and returned to the station only to be informed of the train's further delay of a couple of hours. We strolled out of the station again, turned right, first right again and into a different café at basement level. We piled in and occupied a table. There weren't enough chairs for all of us, so one of us was on duty going around to replenish the plates, whilst the others ate. When one man had finished, he got up and relieved the one on duty so that he could eat. By now it had become a point of honour almost to eat as much as we could. We proceeded to clear the whole place of food before staggering back to the station.

Eventually the men were en route south for Aberdovey. It was here that a proper routine was established and the next phase of training began in earnest. Colin was accommodated in billets with his close friend, Ken Bartlett, along with friends David Stewart and Robbie Villiers at a house called *Rhiw Awel* in Church Street, Aberdovey. Weapons training became more regular and intensive. The programme was brilliantly well designed, conducted by their skipper Hilton-Jones who married during their time in Aberdovey: 'on the day of his wedding, we laid on special parades for him. Although he was just a few years older than us, we had a tremendous respect for him.'

The training included a good deal of map reading, especially at night, with exercises so the men could become accustomed to finding their way in the dark in unfamiliar surroundings: 'We became extremely familiar with the night time through various exercises. We were taught that the dark was our friend. We had to be confident to operate at night.' A thorough command of reading and interpreting a map was a vital part of the training, including sketching to improve the way which they could assess a landscape. Colin recalls:

It was important to focus on parts of the landscape that would not change, i.e. not churches with spires which could be bombed in war time, or railway lines. Buildings and bridges are usually the first targets to be blown up or damaged. For us, the principal reference was always the actual shape of the land, not the surrounding buildings. We studied a map with its contour lines, were told to move from A to B without being seen from point C where the enemy could be. For cross-country marches, we were given a map, asked to go a certain distance in one direction and then a certain distance in another direction. We had excellent army compasses with compass card floating in oil and a luminous ring which would illuminate the edge, and a prismatic sight which could be hinged up over the top once you had opened the cover of it. The prism would allow us to look through and at the same time see the luminous card with the points of the compass engraved on it. It was possible to take an immediate precise bearing on any principal point you were sighting which was useful at night. We learnt that when taking a bearing, one should also take a back bearing so that when you march off and go down hill and can't see your principal point anymore, you can check by the one you came from. On one particular march, there was a railway by the coast so I was able to take bearings from the bridge. But I got puzzled because every time I took a bearing in a certain direction, it would send me straight out to sea. Surely the instructors did not want me to wade out into the sea? Then I tried again. It was definitely trying to get me to walk out to sea. Then it occurred to me that I was wearing a steel helmet, with a Tommy gun slung across my chest, standing on an iron bridge over a double railway line stretching from horizon to horizon, and this had affected the compass!

During training, 3 Troop developed a special technique which they called the 'squeeze me' technique, as Colin explains:

This was a patrol of six or eight men walking close up to each other. We all had our hands on the shoulder of the man in front of us. In the dark, it made it almost impossible for any passers-by to ascertain how many of us there were. Its dark shadow moving along in black-out conditions could easily pass as a cow. If the person in front saw something suspicious, he would go down. As soon as he went down, everybody else reacted and went down with him. If the person at the back could see something suspicious, he would squeeze the shoulder of the man in front. As soon as he squeezed, it would travel up the line and the front man would drop down the second he felt his shoulder squeezed. Then everyone else would follow suit and go down with him. That was extremely effective. We used to walk through villages at pub closing time in the black-out and would collapse, looking like a heap of sand or stones. There was every chance that some of them had had too much to drink and might think they could do their business against us, but fortunately this danger passed us by!

The men underwent all manner of weapons training. The principal weapons with which they became familiar at the training stage were the Short Lee Enfield Rifle, the Bren light machine gun, the 'Tommy gun' – Thompson Machine Carbine – and the Colt .45 pistol. The men were sent to rifle ranges at Machynlleth from time to time for target practice. For pistol practice, grenade throwing and demolition practice they used the sand dunes at the Dovey (Dyfi) estuary. The explosives used for demolitions were Polar Gelignite, mainly for cutting charges to cut through masts or bridge girders, plastic explosives, Amonal (blasting charges for cratering roads), TNT and Guncotton. Colin explains: 'For a primer, where needed, we used Dry Guncotton. Blocks of Guncotton would have a central bore shaped to receive a round Dry Guncotton (stopper-shaped) primer. That primer would have a smaller, straight bore to fit the detonator which in turn would be set off by fast or slow burning fuses, or electrically. For Gelignite or Plastic Explosive (PE), the type of explosion could be varied by using a primer with detonator, or a detonator without primer. The favourite blast explosive for cratering a road was Amonal.' Using live ammunition was not without its risks as Colin recounts:

A 'defensive' grenade, like the more familiar No.36 grenade (often referred to as the Mills Bomb) has a large lethal radius and sprays lethal metal fragments, so the thrower must take cover.

I had an incident one day with a No.69 Grenade which was a percussion grenade of the 'offensive grenade' type. That means that it can be thrown further than its lethal radius. It produces noise, a blast to knock people over and small plastic fragments. The tape has a weight at the end and, when fully unwound in flight, pulls out the safety pin and it then explodes when it hits something or somebody. On one occasion, I took off the plastic cap and watched in fascination as the tape gradually started to unwind. Suddenly an arm came over my right shoulder. It was that of Captain Hilton-Jones. A finger descended onto the tape to stop it from unwinding any further. His calm voice said, 'you *are* a bloody fool, aren't you'. And I replied, 'yes, sir.' I placed my own finger on the tape so it didn't unwind any further. Then I threw it. It was a close one for me that day, but it is something I never did again.

That incident was not the only close shave with weaponry for Colin. The various Troops of No.10 Commando were based in the coastal towns of North Wales; No.3 Troop being the southernmost at Aberdovey, the French of No.1 Troop the most northerly at Criccieth. Commando Headquarters was at Harlech and the Troops took it in turn to provide a headquarters guard, moving into a small barracks building at Harlech for a week or two at a time. Since 3 Troop did not have a national anthem, they adopted *Men of Harlech* as theirs. They manned several sentry posts, including one at the entrance to the castle, which Colin admits felt very romantic:

At one time, the sentry posts of fellow Commando Mac Franklin and myself were within view of each other, and we used to conduct conversations by semaphore signals which was good practice. Every morning we had a parade and inspection, and one morning I was a bit late and just made the parade, sneaking into line with my Tommy gun cocked ready for weapons inspection. But there was no weapons inspection that morning, so when we were dismissed I stuck my gun into the corner of the guardroom and went out. When I came back in time for my turn of sentry duty, I picked up my gun and attached the loaded magazine without noticing that I had not uncocked it. And I had my forefinger inside the trigger guard, and allowed the weight of the gun to rest on it! A burst of three rounds went off, and the first grazed under my friend Ken Bartlett's lower lip. He was lying on his side, and I had been standing at the end of his bed where he was resting after his earlier turn of duty as guard commander. Fortunately the second and third rounds went wide.

I cannot begin to describe what I felt like and what might have happened. The least consequence I expected was to be 'returned to unit' after a spell in a military prison. But when I was brought before our colonel, he proved very lenient. He made allowance for our having been in the Pioneer Corps and unused to weapons. He had had an excellent report about me from my troop commander, felt that after this lesson I would no doubt be more careful in future, and let me off with a reprimand. I owe a debt of gratitude to Colonel Lister. And Ken, generous as ever, did not hold it against me, continued to treat me like a younger brother, and we stayed best friends. He was in hospital for more than two weeks, and the only thing he was worried about was that the scar might spoil his embouchure. He was an oboist, a professional musician, but mercifully it did not interfere with his ability to play the instrument – but he had a small, elegant scar under his lip to the end of his life.

There was one member of 3 Troop about whom a whole series of legends began to grow at this time. It concerned 'Nobby' Kendal (Knobloch), with whom Claus spent a great deal of time:

He was little older than most of us, a corporal in our 87 Company. He was a bit sensitive about his Jewish appearance and very bald. By trade he was an international lawyer, an intellectual with authority and presence. His language tended to be rather meticulous. He was tough, a very good soldier, but he had a knack of doing things in an odd way even if he was right. He was the only man I ever knew who re-assembled a Bren gun the wrong way – and it's not supposed to be possible. A hammer and chisel was used to get the barrel out again! When we were at Aberdovey and had a new intake of recruits, Nobby was asked to give them a lecture on weapons in an interview room in the small Town Hall. He was supposed to talk about the Colt pistol, but since he had forgotten his pistol, someone came from the guard room and lent him another weapon. He asked the new intake: 'what's the first thing we do when picking up any sort of weapon? That's right, safety precautions. With a pistol, it is very simple. All you have to do is slide the action back, look through the ejection opening into chamber to make sure there isn't a cartridge in it. Now the weapon is perfectly safe.'

BANG!

And there was a small hole in the ceiling. He had forgotten there was a loaded magazine in the handle and as soon as he pulled it back and let go, he charged one of the cartridges into the chamber. On another occasion when we were first issued with these weapons, we tried them out in our section of the sand dunes at Aberdovey. Nobby adopted a duellist's posture with one fist behind his back in the position of taking aim. He then bobbed up and down, flexing his knees, pointing the weapon straight behind him. Everyone flopped down and took cover. When asked what on earth he was doing, he said he was 'feeling-in the weapon'.

Whatever the men learnt was always interspersed with rigourous physical training. They had to maintain a very high degree of physical fitness which was always exacting and exerting. Part of the fitness training included expeditions to Snowdonia for rock climbing:

We had wonderful times around Lake Ogwen and Idwal. We learnt our basic rock-climbing on the Idwal slabs which are excellent climbing country. One incident happened towards the end of a trip to Snowdonia when Ernie Lawrence fell out of Hollytree Wall, beyond the Idwal Slabs. I threw a rope around me and rushed up the Idwal Slabs, and suddenly realised, 'by goodness, I can do that!' Not clinging to the rock but standing well off it, I instinctively rushed up it without even thinking. If I had hesitated, I couldn't have done it. I suddenly realised that all the training had had some effect. By the time I got to the top, a team was already there with a stretcher to get Lawrence down. He wasn't badly hurt, but had to be taken to Bangor Hospital. From time to time, we would go to the hospital to visit him and other comrades who had been injured during training.

One exercise during their time at Aberdovey remains vivid for Colin:

It was a night exercise during which we set out in the evening over the hills to Tal-y-Llin lake, and then skirted its north shore to a path ascending Cader Idris, a high mountain in Snowdonia. The weather steadily deteriorated, until the drizzle became a steady rain in a high wind. By now it was pitch dark, and we could hardly see our hands in front of our faces. It must have been well after midnight when we reached the summit. We tried to find the beginning of a path down the northern side, towards Dolgelly (as we then spelt it), which was said to be marked with coloured sand – but there was no way we could see coloured sand in the dark, not to mention the rain and thick mist. So we started down the most likely place which turned out not to be a path, but a stream. We progressed as carefully as we could, until we came to a rocky edge on which to sit in the rushing water, unable to feel anything under our feet, and then kick off in the hope of landing on something solid. The waterfalls were the most sustained showerbath I have ever experienced. As dawn broke we made it as far as the scree and rocks at the bottom, and then marched to a yard by the railway line to Barmouth, where we were drawn up to be inspected by an elderly, retired General. I was standing behind Mac Franklin and saw the muzzle of his rifle trembling to and fro as he presented arms. The General walked along the front rank, stopping at times to ask silly question of our wet, cold and exhausted troop members. He asked Mac 'Are you wet?'

'Yes sir!' answered Mac.

'Do you like being wet?'

'No Sir!' How Mac managed to keep his mischievous humour in check I don't know. Our weapons had become red-rusty overnight. That no-one got hurt in this blind descent, or broke an ankle in the rough scree, is a miracle. And under the circumstances, the Skipper allowed us to be taken back to Aberdovey by lorry instead of marching down the coast road, as originally planned.

The instructors devised special missions, one of which was to penetrate an RAF base at Towyn, six miles from Aberdovey, to retrieve specific information without being detected. This particular operation was so successful that the RAF authorities were none the wiser that the commandos had ever penetrated the base. Another challenge was given to 3 Troop:

It was triggered by a challenge from officers of other units who dared our Skipper Hilly (Hilton-Jones) to demonstrate that we were as good as he had claimed. Our troop was taken near the tip of the Pwllheli peninsula in North Wales and left there, as though we had been enemy troops dropped by parachute. We had to make our way to a river across the base of the peninsula, cross it and simulate the blowing-up of a prominent radio mast on the other side by leaving coloured sand in its base as pretend-explosives. We carried the sand in our ammunition pouches. There were conditions: we were not allowed to use or purloin any transport, we had to wear our green berets so we could be identified, the population was told to look out for us and all available Army,

RAF Regiment, Police and Home Guard units in the area were to try and catch us. Once spotted, we were declared dead.

It seemed an impossible task, but Hilly accepted the dare. We used all our skills and all available cover, split into small groups to move invisibly across country, and avoided roads, habitations and people. The trickiest task was to get over roads running across our direction of travel unseen by hiding in ditches and hedges until an 'enemy' patrol had just passed and then nip over before the next (or any people or traffic) appeared. The organisers of our opponents timed our probable rate of progress and, at given intervals, moved their 'defensive' lines further back to reinforce those we would not yet have crossed. So our task became more and more difficult as the defenders grew ever denser. Also, we had to move fast to beat a time limit that had been set to finish before dark. And yet, we very nearly did it! We did in fact reach the river which we had hoped to cross, but the defenders had now pulled all their personnel back into a practically unbroken line, standing shoulder-to-shoulder along the river bank. There was no way around, and we were all caught; frankly, we did not even try, exhausted as we were after our cross-country march of some 20 miles against such odds. It gave us great confidence, and enhanced our reputation.

One particularly memorable training period away from Aberdovey was to HMS *Tormentor*, a shore establishment of the Royal Navy near Portsmouth on the south coast of England. It was dedicated to landing craft operations and it was here that Colin underwent two weeks of boat training on different kinds of landing craft:

We underwent a fair amount of landing and boating training in the wooden speedboats known as LCPs (Landing Craft Personnel), manned with naval personnel. We learnt how to drive them but they went out of fashion because the LCA (Landing Craft Assault) soon became our proper dedicated vehicle. They were very good – fairly low in the water, open top oblong, with practically no draft. It meant we could get really close into a rocky coast. The main part had three very low benches where we crouched, astride them. As soon as we landed on a beach during exercises, the crew threw out an anchor and the ramp would go down. The two armoured doors at the front would open and we would rush out as quickly as possible in the order: centre bench, right hand bench, left hand bench. On leaving the landing craft, the important thing was not to bunch, but spread out and run for cover beyond the beach. We would rush up the beach into the hinterland and then disappear into the dunes. The lack of such training cost the Americans very dear in the D-Day landings on Omaha Beach in 1944 when US soldiers rushed on shore, but tried to take cover by just lying down under the German machine gun posts which were raking their fire across them. The Americans had enormous casualties and losses that day: ninety-four per cent on landing. Fortunately I have never been in a situation where we had great casualties on landing during our commando raids in action.

Our exercises from HMS *Tormentor* were aimed at landing on the Isle of Wight. We would fire off lots of ammunition, partly to encourage us and give us confidence in our own firepower. That way we experienced the amount of firepower that we could use against the enemy to discourage in-coming fire. The main point of these exercises was to approach the coast, but quietly so as not draw attention to ourselves, successfully land and then use ropes to climb the cliffs.

During their time at HMS *Tormentor*, the men were accommodated in private billets, as was always their privilege as commandos. Days off were spent around Portsmouth, often frequently in the pubs on street corners. 'By the time we finally got into Portsmouth itself, we were already in quite a merry mood!' After the two weeks at *Tormentor*, intensive training continued at Aberdovey under the guidance of Captain Hilton-Jones. Regular training included speed marches of five miles out, five miles back with full equipment:

It was demanding but we maintained the level of fitness and self-confidence which we needed to be successful commandos. We were given exercises which we never thought possible. In achieving the seemingly impossible, we enhanced our self-confidence. We might never need it in action, but we had the knowledge that we could do it if required. We also had rudimentary intelligence training and learnt as much as we could about German army practice and battle order. This was so that in action, when we came across bodies of dead German soldiers, we could identify their rank and unit, and what kind of documents to try and retrieve from them.

The time came for the men to be detached from 3 Troop and attached to other commando units, including the Royal Marine Commandos, for action abroad. Members of 3 Troop served in all European theatres of war, including the invasion of Italy and Sicily in the summer of 1943 and the D-Day landings in Normandy in June 1944. Casualties for 3 Troop were high.

As German-speakers and being highly trained, the men of 3 Troop brought specialist knowledge and skills to whichever unit they were seconded. They were able to crack open safes, pick locks, scale walls, kill a person silently with their bare hands, use explosives, assemble fuses and detonators, and successfully carry out night time raids. With an intimate knowledge of German military command structure, they were able to carry out night operations and raids effectively. They were the first servicemen in the British forces to be issued with rubber-soled boots instead of the usual hob-nailed ones, enabling silent movement during operations. Some of what they learnt in training might never be used in action, but they had to be prepared. The troop went on parachute training, but Colin was no longer with them at that point. With his training now complete, Colin was ready for action:

We never considered ourselves brave. That was the forte of the bomber pilots and parachutists. We were just doing what we had to do to defeat Adolf Hitler and his evil regime. Because of the nature of our training, we knew what we were in for. None of us really expected to survive the war, especially our raids behind enemy lines. We knew the risks, but I could not sit back and let others fight this war. This was my war.

CHAPTER 6

The Invasion of Sicily

I n May 1943, Colin was amongst the first group of four German-speakers to be detached from 3 Troop to No. 40 Royal Marine Commando and No. 41 RM Commando. Colin was attached to 40 Commando with Hugh Miles (Levin); Paul Streeten (Hornig) and Mac Franklin (Frank) to 41 Commando. At the time 40 Commando was based on the south-west coast of Scotland, training with 41 Commando in final preparation for active service abroad. Colin joined A Troop of 40 Commando for assault landing practice on the beaches of Troon and Irvine on the south-west coast of Scotland (Ayrshire, now part of Strathclyde). 'It was an exceedingly wet time. We trained on enormous stretches of beach in the heavy rain and were far wetter from the rain than during the actual exercises in the water! We were billeted at Troon in private accommodation. My unit was under the command of Captain Ephraims who was one of the finest and most popular officers I ever came across. They were one of the two original marine commandos that had been recruited from volunteers from all over the marines. The later ones were RM battalions converted into commandos.' Colin remained in Scotland until embarkation onto a convoy on the Clyde, bound for action overseas. At this juncture none of the men knew for certain their intended destination. That same month, Colin embarked at Greenock onto the troopship *Devonshire* which had been converted as a troop carrier. It was very crowded:

We were issued with tropical kit and in the spirit of the time, we tried to out-guess what was happening. We said, 'Ah, the tropical kit is to fool the enemy.

We're sure to be going to Norway.' We were security conscious and aware that enemy agents might watch ports to report back what units were embarking for what destinations. We embarked on the *Devonshire*; were then instructed to disembark, and finally to re-embark. We never really knew which embarkation was the real thing until one day we actually set sail. Then we were part of a huge convoy of ships with a piper playing us out as we passed through the Clyde. It was all very impressive. As the ship passed out, I remember an enthusiastic old chap in highland garb on shore, waving his greetings and blessing as the ship passed close by. It was a great encouragement and added to the excitement of our journey.

It was many days later that Brigadier Laycock, Chief of Combined Operations, informed the men that they were going to be part of what was then the biggest landing and combined operation yet undertaken – the invasion of Sicily, codenamed *Operation Husky*. This was eleven months before D-Day and the Allied invasion of Normandy of 6 June 1944. The convoy headed in a westerly direction, turned south, then eastwards. Below decks, conditions were cramped but bearable, with men sleeping on the iron floor, and more in two layers of hammocks, almost touching. 'It was,' recalls Colin, 'debatable whether in an emergency we would have been able to get out in a hurry.' Now as part of the marines, Colin had the privilege of being treated like the other sea-going marines. He was given duties on the anti-aircraft gun emplacements:

We became gun crews, but with virtually no training. The anti-aircraft gun emplacement allocated to our group housed a Bofors light AA gun in the centre of a stepped amphitheater. The gunner fitted his shoulders into two curved shoulder pieces with a strap across his back, so he could aim the gun by traversing and elevating it as he danced round, and up-and-down the steps. We took it in turns to act as gunner; the other members of the crew stood by with loaded magazines to replace empty ones. But we never saw enemy aircraft, so it did not come to that. There were vertical tubular guards fitted in strategic places to fend off the barrel of the gun if a gunner, his full attention concentrated on an attacking aircraft, might follow it round too enthusiastically and accidentally saw off a mast or pepper the bridge of our own ship with cannon shells. We carried out normal naval watches of four hours on, four hours off, except for the two-hour 'dog watches'. The irregular sleeping periods took some getting used to, but on the other hand the privilege of sunning ourselves in our own private eyrie near the bridge was a great luxury, while the crowds below were shoved from one place to another by 'Now Hear This' orders blaring from the tannoy while sections of the decks were hosed and swabbed down.

Fortunately we were not attacked during our journey towards the Mediterranean, although sometimes at night we heard the thump of depth charges which were aimed at U-boats. Eventually the convoy passed through the straits of Gibraltar which was dramatic for us because on the one side there was the fortress of Gibraltar and the Rock, in complete darkness, and on the other side were the bright lights of Tangier. It was impressive to see because by now we had been so used to the enforced black-outs in Britain.

In the Bay of Tunis the convoy joined an ever-increasing armada of vessels which stretched from horizon to horizon. On 10 July 1943 it set course for the south-eastern tip of Sicily, due to land close to Cape Passero, near Pachino, passing Malta in the far distance on the way. 40 Commando with 3 and 41 Commandos were to spearhead the invasion of Sicily.

The weather started to deteriorate markedly. The severe weather was to the attackers' advantage as they learnt later, because German units had been withdrawn from the area in Sicily where they were due to land. It was felt that no one could possibly land in such conditions. But also, there were a number of successful decoy intelligence operations which led the Germans to believe that the landings were to be in Sardinia, or even Greece, anywhere but where they were actually going to take place.[24] The day before landing, the weather took a further dramatic turn for the worse with enormous high seas. As they got closer to their landing area, after nightfall, the LCAs (Landing Craft Assault) were swung outboard in their electric derricks, and lowered level with the deck for the men to board them. Each LCA held thirty-six men and naval personnel. Then they were lowered away and, as they hit the water, unhooked so they could proceed from there under their own power:

> It was a dramatic journey – the sea was extremely rough, the waves formidable and there was a danger of the landing craft capsizing. I was sitting on the left hand bench about half way along. The man in front had the radio sets which I promised to help him get ashore if we had a wet landing. It was vital that the radio equipment did not get wet. The sea became so rough that we had to sit with legs inwards and I jammed my pack beneath the gangway to be lodged in place. The dark horizon disappeared, and all I saw was a sky full of stars. By now it wasn't cloudy. We were tossed about and the other horizon rose up. But as we entered the bay, the sea suddenly went as calm as a millpond. It was very surreal. I can still remember the smell of warm tropical vegetation coming over the sea and the sound of Cicadas as we approached the shore.

The men approached the coast. They cruised for a while and formed up with the various landing craft and anti-aircraft boats which could give covering fire. Some carried rockets. In dark waters in the middle of the night they were not visible to the enemy. They were about to be the first wave of an invasion force at that point on Sicily, landing after some naval gun preparations beforehand, one of which was ironically provided by HMS *Anson*.[25] The Italians were hiding in carefully camouflaged pill boxes. They started to fire wildly with machine guns using tracer bullets. 'They sensed that something was happening,' says Colin, 'but not exactly what. The tracer fire allowed us to see where they were firing from.' The commandos and other incoming forces came under some fire but suffered few casualties. Most losses were experienced by the Italians. Grenades were thrown at the haystacks setting them on fire and making short work of the Italian defences. Concern that German Tiger units were operating in the vicinity were soon quashed as they had withdrawn. All up and down the Sicilian coast, landings were taking place: along the east and south coast; the latter landings not being so easy:

> The Americans suffered quite a few casualties on landing. It was a full-scale invasion. There were also parachute drops of British troops. We got ashore with hardly any casualties. We felt tense but not fear because we were too busy getting on with the job. We were also very tired because we hadn't had much sleep before landing. There had been last minute aerial photographs coming in and we had had to study the area we were going to attack. The adrenalin ran high during the course of the landings. We did not land on the beach but a little way off on a false beach which was a hill of sand under the water which dropped away again. If the assault craft grounded on a false beach, the naval crew would put out an anchor at the stern to pull the craft off again, so as not to risk it getting stuck fast. One had to get into deepening water before gaining the shallows: a wet landing. The wireless sets had to be lifted high to keep them dry – that was my job. That night we had rather a wet landing. We waded in up to our chests. Major Hellings was the first to go, a short squat man, who said: 'Right, follow me!' He stepped off the ramp, into the water but we could only see his tin helmet! Fortunately neither he nor anyone else drowned.

Colin waded out of the water with the other men and up the beach. They split into three columns. Two went along the coast mopping up defences either side of the landing spot; the third went inland. Colin was with the third column. It was still pitch dark; dawn was a couple of hours away. Then came a terrible moment:

> There was a bit of movement in front of us, so some of our men started firing. The shrill scream of a woman penetrated the night air. The officers and NCOs

were doing nothing to stop the shooting, so I shouted: 'Cease fire! You are shooting at civilians.' I was only a private at the time and had no authority to give orders, but nobody was doing anything. They stopped firing, but by that time, a woman had been mortally wounded. There was no time to stop. We proceeded inland. I helped with languages, could speak no Italian so managed as best I could. As we passed a farm, people started to come out curious at us. I told them to get back inside and close the doors. We did not come across other enemy activity except a bit of mortar fire.

Eventually we returned to the beach where we had landed and where everyone was now forming up into the perimeter to allow other units to land after us. Then there was a mistaken fire fight between two Allied parties. Both had taken Italian prisoners who were only too pleased to have surrendered because it meant their war was over. The prisoners were being herded back to the beach, quite relieved and chattering amongst themselves. Each group found these Italians coming towards them, speaking a foreign language, so they opened fire. The others started shooting back until someone remembered to shout the password which was for that night: 'Desert rats'. The reply came back: 'Kill Italians' and the firing stopped. It was on the beachhead that night that I discovered that olive trees are very uncomfortable to sleep under because their roots are on the surface and very knobbly. It was a warm night, so I started to nod off to sleep. Then I was woken with a start by a horrible scream, followed by a snorting sound, only to discover several mules around. I learnt that the mules were used by the forces to transport supplies and weapons.

After an uncomfortable night on the beach, the following morning Colin and the men began their advance with other units, by which time some of the mules had been commandeered by marines. Carts were also used to transport guns and ammunition with the mules to pull them. By now a whole Canadian field hospital had set up near the beach. Deeply concerned about the family of the woman who had been shot the previous night, Colin paid a visit to the farm:

We were very tired but I made it my point to visit the farm. I knocked on the door, went into the family room and took off my helmet as a mark of respect. There in front of me was the girl aged about twenty laid out on the table. I went up to the mother, dressed head to toe in black, shook her by the hand and expressed my condolences. But she was inconsolable. I did the same with the father who was much more accepting and indicated, 'I'm sure you meant no harm. This happens in war time.' My presence there that day was my way of indicating that we were not monsters, but sympathetic human beings. All the time I was doing that I was acutely aware of the fact that there were four young men behind me. We were in Sicily where blood feuds and exaction of revenge are not entirely unknown. I turned and shook each of their hands in turn. We parted friends and I hope that it helped to sow a little goodwill. On the whole, the population was extremely welcoming. Whenever we patrolled inland and passed a farm, out came glasses of wine in welcome.

There was some military activity during the advance inland. Colin and his comrades were being mortared. One of the lieutenants was injured and had to taken back to the Canadian field hospital on the beach. With no stretchers to hand, Colin and his comrades borrowed a ladder from a nearby farm to put the wounded man on. 'Four of us then took him back,' recalls Colin, 'over rough ground and through the fields, back to the beach. It was very heavy going and extremely hot. The ladder was hard on our shoulders, but we finally managed to get him to the hospital.' Then Colin returned the ladder to the farm annex from where he had taken it. Ever courteous and considerate for the local population, he knocked on the door and walked into a great communal dining room where the whole family was at dinner:

> A girl with curly black hair and deep black eyes looked fascinatingly at this British soldier standing in front of them. I wanted to thank them for the loan of the ladder and I said, 'thank you' but could not remember the word for 'ladder'. I made a stair-climbing motion with my fingers. And the father of the family piped up, '*Ah! La Scala!*'
>
> I replied, '*Si, la scala, do-re-mi-fa-sol!*': the musical scale meaning ladder, as I might have known. So we all laughed.
>
> In general, our relations seemed to be quite good. They looked on us as liberators because the Sicilians were not fond of the Italians. We were not treated in a hostile way by the Sicilians.

It was whilst on Sicily that Colin had two near shaves with death in one day. He had been given a message to take to another unit which was some distance away from the beach where he had landed. He made his way to the said location to find that there was no unit there. He then passed a military policeman who informed him that the unit had moved off but he did not know where, but thought to be in the direction of Pachino. Colin trudged off towards Pachino and was shortly joined by another soldier who was also trying to find the same unit. Being desperately tired as they all were, the other soldier decided to crawl under a burned-out tank for a sleep. Colin carried on until he almost reached Pachino.

The young Claus Ascher with his father, Bad Homburg

Above: Reichswehrminister Noske with Curt Ascher and German officers, 1919

Left: Mathilde Ascher (née Ruyter), opera singer, 1911

Above: Curt Ascher at Reichwehr sport event, 1919

Right: Curt Ascher, Colin's father, Reichswehrministerum, 1919

Above left: Claus Ascher with his father, Berlin 1922

Above right: Playing with father's walking stick

Left: As a German schoolboy in Bad Homburg, 1931

Postcard sent by Curt Ascher to his family from Dachau concentration camp, 3 October 1937

Absender: Curt Ascher

Konzentrationslager Dachau

Folgende Anordnungen sind beim Schriftverkehr mit Gefangenen zu beachten:

1.) Jeder Schutzhaftgefangene darf in der Woche einen Brief oder eine Karte von seinen Angehörigen empfangen und an sie absenden. Die Briefe an die Gefangenen müssen gut lesbar geschrieben sein und dürfen nur 15 Zeilen auf einer Seite enthalten. Gestattet ist nur ein Briefbogen normaler Größe. Briefumschläge müssen ungefüttert sein. In einem Briefe dürfen nur 5 Briefmarken à 12 Pfg. beigelegt werden. Alles andere ist verboten und unterliegt der Beschlagnahme. Postkarten haben 10 Zeilen.
2.) Geldsendungen sind gestattet.
3.) Zeitungen sind gestattet, dürfen aber nur durch die Poststelle des K. L. Dachau bestellt werden.
4.) Pakete dürfen nicht geschickt werden, da die Gefangenen im Lager alles kaufen können.

Alle Post, die diesen Anforderungen nicht entspricht, geht an die Absender zurück. Ist kein Absender bekannt, so wird sie vernichtet.

Der Lagerkommandant.

The only letter sent from Curt Ascher to his family from Dachau, censored by the Gestapo

1 Reisedecke

1 Jackett

1 Knickerbockerhose

1 Ärmelpullover

2 Hemden

1 langes Unterzeug

2 kurze   "

30 Taschentücher

1 Schlafanzug

Wasch- und Toilettesachen

1 Schuhputz – Necessaire

Nähzeug

1 Kleiderbürste

2 Kravatten

Schnürsenkel

1 Taschenlampe

1 Mappe, darin:

Photografien

1 Federmäppchen mit Bleistift, Federhalter und Gummi.

1 Bleistiftspitzer

The list of belongings Colin took out of Germany when he emigrated to England in February 1939

On leave from the Pioneer
Corps, Liverpool 1941

Colin Anson, 1946

Army Paybook in the Pioneer Corps under original name Claus Ascher

Army Paybook for Special Forces under new name Colin Anson

Training on the Idwal Slabs, Snowdonia, Wales

Colin in 3 Troop, No. 10 Inter-Allied Commando

Members of 3 Troop. Front row, left to right: unknown, Mac Franklin; back row, left to right: unknown, Shelley, Sayers

Members of 3 Troop. From left to right: Wallen, Gordon, Nicholls, unknown, Mac Franklin, Fuller

Commandos on the beach, Albania, 1944

3 Troop at Aberdovey, 1943

List of those pictured at Aberdovey:
1. Graham; 2. Aitcheson; 3. Masters; 4. Hamilton; 5. Tenant; 6. Hepworth, W.; 7. Garvin; 8. Naughton; 9. Streeten; 10. Douglas; 11. Carson (?); 12. Moody; 13. Scott; 14. Sayers; 15. Laddy; 16. Gilbert; 17. Franklin; 18. Farr; 19. Long; 20. Ross; 21. Nelson; 22. Anson; 23. Hudson; 24. Shelly; 25. Lewis; 26. Anderson; 27. Merton; 28. Saunders; 29. Griffiths; 30. Envers; 31. Bentley; 32. Harris; 33. Unknown; 34. Marshal; 35. Kingsley; 36. Stewart; 37. Seymour; 38. Arlen; 39. Drew; 40. Grey; 41. Barnes; 42. Fenton; 43. Nichols; 44. Bartlet; 45. Miles; 46. Andrews (?); 47. Wallen; 48. Turner; 49. Mason; 50. O'Neil; 51. Streets; 52. McGregor; 53. Davis; 54. Hilton-Jones; 55. Emmett; 60. Kendall; 61. Villiars; 62. Wells.

Colin in Rome, 1945

Alice Gross, WAAF

Colin reunited with his mother after the war, Frankfurt

Victory tea for No. 10 Inter-Allied Commando, May 1945. Many members of 3 Troop present.

Above: Colin's engagement to ex-Viennese refugee Alice Gross

Left: Colin with their three children, Barbara, Diana and Edward, on a visit to Bad Homburg

Colin with a T-31
two-seater glider,
Hatfield

Noel Edmunds and
Barbara Cartland
filming with Colin's
aircraft made up to
look like a BAC7

Colin with a comrade in
an aircraft

Memorial to 3 Troop at
Aberdovey, Wales

Colin and Alice in
retirement, 2009

By now the Germans had evacuated the area and there was no unit. He turned around and began trudging all the way back:

I was passing the latitude of the field hospital which was the final point if you were not sure where to go, a central message clearing point. Because I was so tired, I decided to cut across country and down to the beach but I nearly got myself stuck in quicksand. I was still heavily loaded down with ammunition. Being in the quicksand and sinking was a very odd feeling, but I did manage to get out. I gave up on short-cuts, walked around, and then down to the beach where we had first landed. I trudged along the beach to the Canadian field hospital. It was towards morning because I saw the sun rising up towards me. By now I was on my last legs and totally shattered. I made my way to the hospital, by then I had forgotten any message to any unit and to whom it should have been delivered. I heard the doctor say: 'he's so exhausted. Give him a stretcher and a blanket. He's half crazy with fatigue.'

I lay out on the stretcher and covered myself with the blanket. The next thing I was aware of was somebody in bright sunlight taking the blanket off my face and saying: 'But he isn't dead. That's Anson. I know him.' It was Sergeant Angel of 40 Commando speaking. When people died in action in Sicily, this particular field hospital put the dead on stretchers with a blanket over their face, then took them outside and placed them in a long row. I discovered that they had put some dead soldiers next to me! Whilst I took out my rations and started having breakfast, they took the rest of the dead away and buried them with the padre saying a few words. I would have had a rough, untimely awakening! That was the first time, but not the last, that I more or less attended my own funeral.

The first time during the war that Colin discovered a dead soldier was in Sicily as he was making his way through a field of maize:

The maize was fairly high and provided excellent cover. I was making my way to our position when I nearly trod on him. He was an Italian soldier lying on his back, looking composed, except his mouth was closed with a perfect round hole in it. This was where the bullet had gone in. He was a lone dead body. The fields were not covered with dead bodies as they were in the First World War on the Western Front. Our war was so much more mobile.

A substantial part of Sicily was now properly under Allied control. Colin started to move with 40 Commando up the east coast. He has snapshot memories from this period of the war. They arrived in Syracuse, which had already been taken by forces that had landed in that area. They settled on a green strip in the middle of a dual carriageway:

> We were eating our rations, but it was terribly difficult not to give away our food to the children asking for biscuits 'for mama and papa'. It was also at this time that I heard that a U-boat had arrived in the port of Syracuse. It had dived again so as not to be visible, had managed to go through the defensive anti-submarine nets which had gaps so that Sicilian vessels could pass through. When the U-boat surfaced, they found British soldiers grinning down at them. It must have been quite a surprise.

Colin was exhausted from days en route, moving to Syracuse, about thirty miles. He had been dismissed for the day because they were not advancing further until the following morning. He entered a hotel near the harbour, found a room and promptly fell sleep. It was towards evening when he woke: 'I re-joined my comrades and they asked: "Where were you during the air raid?" There had been a heavy raid and I had slept right through it. The rest had done me good and thereafter I was much more alert.'

They then advanced on Augusta. Comforts were few, with no tents for shelter. A road bridge over a small river in the Catania plain, over-towered by Mt Etna, was being tenaciously defended by the enemy. It was difficult to approach, so it was decided that they should board fast assault ships to make a landing in Catania to the rear of the Germans. Colin and his comrade boarded the *Queen Emma* which in peacetime was a Dutch Channel packet. It was very smart, now adapted to carry assault boats. It was towards evening. The *Queen Emma* was the furthest from the shore in Augusta Bay and as such was responsible for laying the smoke screen to protect the other ships from attack. The onshore breeze blew over the shipping in the bay but left the *Queen Emma* rather visible. That night it came under unexpected sustained air attack from Stukas, German dive-bombers, causing a great number of casualties. The ship's doctor and commando medical officer were both killed. The ship was littered with the dead and injured. Only the commando medical sergeant and his team survived to deal with all the casualties:

> The date I always remember. It was 17 July 1943. At the time of the attack, we were busy preparing for landing behind German positions. A lot of our people were maimed or killed because down in the hold, one of the near-misses from a Stuka which did the most damage caused the ammunition to go off. It was this that caused all the casualties. That night it was so hot and stuffy below, that I had slung my hammock on the well deck, towards the rear of the

vessel. Once the attack started, I rolled out of my hammock and lay flat on the deck. When this particular hit came, I did not hear it. Although it was a near miss, it made the ship roll to a fair degree. The force of it knocked me out, but not for very long. I saw a swirling grey background and I could hear the rushing of the sea. It can't have lasted very long because I was aware of the ship not going completely over, but beginning to right itself. A great deal of water came on board. I tried without success to blow up my Mae West inflatable lifebelt, because on my right side I seemed to be rather paralysed. I couldn't move my arm and my leg would not function properly. I finally managed to get myself upright and also asked a nearby marine: 'Can I come in with you? I can't seem to blow up my Mae West.' It was then that the ship completely righted itself.

I was then able to move a little more normally. I passed the casualties and tried to make myself useful. I found a marine called Wood, whom we nicknamed Timber, from A Troop. He had shrapnel in his abdomen. I pulled him into a gangway to get him out of the direct path of the splinters raining down on us. I gave him a sip from my water bottle, but I really should not have done it to someone with shrapnel in his bowels in case he needed an operation. Still the attacks continued. When I heard another Stuka coming down with its characteristic siren noise (caused by dive brake and high-revving engine and propeller), I took off my helmet and put it over Timber's face to protect him. Fortunately the Stuka did not drop anything. It pulled out of its dive and flew away. It was then, and only then, whilst I had my helmet off that I noticed blood dripping onto my arm. I thought nothing more of it and put my helmet back on.

It was a terrifying night. The air attacks continued until first light. The next morning, Colin went to see the medical sergeant to ask for a bandage, explaining that he had slashed his head somehow during one of the raids. It was at that moment that he removed his helmet to the shock of the medical sergeant:

He looked terribly serious and told me to sit down on the floor in the corner, with the instruction not to move. I thought it was very odd for him to make such a fuss over me with a small scratch. Odd, especially after all the terrible injuries he had had to deal with all through the night. Then I began to feel rather strange, sick and faint. A marine wanted to give me some rum and I just about managed to fend him off. Then I fainted, came around but did not feel too bad. Presently some boats came alongside us to evacuate the wounded. I was left sitting there whilst they took the others away. It so happened that I was amongst the last to be put on a stretcher and lowered over the side of our ship into a boat to be taken ashore. I thought this was understandable because they had to deal with the most serious cases first. I later learnt from the commando medical sergeant that in fact they had left me until last because I was not expected to survive the night. My brain was visible where part of my skull had been shot. When the hit had occurred, a piece of shrapnel had penetrated through my helmet and into my skull.

Colin was taken ashore and then transported by ambulance to 151 Light Field Ambulance Unit, which had set up on Sicily in an olive grove. It consisted of two three-tonne lorries, complete with a full-size operating theatre at the back; the other with all the gear, and a tent attached with room for a dozen beds. It was staffed by Canadian nurses in ice-blue overalls:

> They saved many lives because they had the necessary equipment to take quick action. In my case, I was put in a bed, and at my feet there was a lorry marked with a red cross. I felt so comfortable between crisp white sheets but began to feel rather drowsy. The Red Cross on that lorry began to get smaller and smaller, and further and further away. Then I blacked out. I saw afterwards on the field card around my neck, that I had stopped breathing for half an hour. I had been kept alive by external heart massage, by doctors using compression of the ribcage. In that mobile hospital, the medical team performed a delicate brain operation, fishing bone splinters out of my brain. The bomb splinter which had done the damage was still there. The shrapnel had lodged itself inside the skull in the back of the head where it still is to this day! I have seen in recent X-rays that it has shrunk a fair bit and is now quite small. All the ragged edges have smoothed over the years. I know that from comparison with early X-rays. When I finally came around from the operation, I found that I was wearing a plaster cast helmet. Some fellow patients signed their names on it and one of them drew a dagger badge on the front.

After the operation, Colin was transported by hospital ship to Tripoli in North Africa for approximately two weeks. It had spacious bunks on gimbals (sophisticated pivots) such that if the ship rolled it did not affect the patient. Next to Colin was a young German paratrooper. Although they had been on opposing sides of the war, the paratrooper seemed pleased to have someone next to him who could speak German, as Colin recalls:

> We chatted quite a bit. He told me how he had been hung about like Christmas trees when they had jumped. He was cheerful and good company, but when they came to renew his dressing, I realised that he had been very badly

wounded by a bullet entering below one of his buttocks and exiting midriff. We continued to chat, then he said to me that he was rather uncomfortable and asked, 'Could you get someone to give me something?' I said to the sister: 'He would like some relief'. She replied, 'No, impossible. In his state of health and the way he has lost blood, I couldn't take the responsibility.' The paratrooper and I continued to talk, and he got rougher and rougher. Again I asked the nurse for something to relieve his pain. She gave the same reply. Then a bit later, the paratrooper said: 'just tell them to give me something – anything. It is on my responsibility. If I don't wake up again, I don't care. Just ask them for something for the pain, please.' I asked the sister very urgently. She looked at him with raised eyebrows and said, 'Okay, but on his responsibility then.' She came back with a syringe and gave him a shot. He said to me, 'I don't think this is working.' Then before he could say another word, he was in a deep sleep. The sister came back with a little smile and said to me: 'Do you know what that was I gave him? Distilled water. I couldn't have dreamt of giving him anything really strong.' I couldn't help smiling to myself. That was the last I saw of him. When we were unloaded at Tripoli, he may have been taken to the same hospital, but I did not see him again.

How did Colin feel about the German paratrooper? After all he was the enemy and a hated Nazi soldier at that. His response: 'Anyone in that situation knows from experience how difficult it is to resist the urge to fraternise. You are both in the same situation and there is a strong feeling of affinity and sympathy. Once the fighting has stopped, then you no longer have a personal animosity towards each other. I came across that quite a lot during the war.'

After a while, Colin was registered as an outpatient and issued with a set of blues – the hospital uniform for patients which consisted blue trousers and jacket, white shirt and scarlet tie. He borrowed a Topee (pith helmet or sun helmet) to protect his head wound from the strong North African sun. It was still July 1943. By now he was well enough to take a day trip into Tripoli and look around, which he did. It was whilst Colin was in the hospital in Tripoli that he came across someone he thought was a former mate from 87 Company Pioneer Corps who was sitting one day in the gardens of the grounds:

He was sitting on a bench. I walked passed him and nodded. I gave no other sign of recognition. We were trained to respect if someone did not wish to be recognised. I then sat next to him and made a routine remark. There was no kind of response. Then I looked over both shoulders and made sure we were not overheard and said: 'Hello, don't you remember me?'

'No, should I?' he answered.

'Does the number 87 mean anything to you?'

'I'm afraid not, should it?'

I said to him: 'You're Baron, aren't you?'

He replied, 'No, my name is Srebrov.' He came from Romania and was not Baron but I have never come across anyone who was so precise a duplicate of someone I know. We parted friends. It was many years later that I saw Baron again after the war. He was visiting North-West London for a couple of weeks and I swear that he looked interchangeably the same as Srebrov. A really bizarre incident.

After about two weeks in hospital at Tunis, Colin was to be transferred to a specialist surgical unit at the 15th Scottish General Hospital in Cairo. There were hours of waiting in the entrance hall of the hospital at Tunis until the flight. He was given a mug of tea and jam sandwich, and a lady came round with a trolley of books. Colin chose a book to read called *Fate Cannot Harm Me*:

The book tells of a man who was crossed in love. On returning from spending years in Africa and on exploration expeditions to try to get over his heartbreak, he is welcomed home by his best friend who gives him a magnificent dinner. Whilst eating they tell each other what they had been doing during those years. In the book, the dinner is described blow by blow, in mouth-watering detail. I read the book during the long waits and the six-hour flight to Cairo – after having had nothing that day but a mug of tea and a jam sandwich at 5 o'clock am. I was getting hungrier and hungrier, reading pages of detailed description about food! In the book, the dinner ended with his best friend confessing that he had married the girl during the jilted suitor's absence abroad – and the title of the book is a quotation which reads: 'Fate cannot harm me – I have dined today!'

For the flight by Dakota plane from Castel Benito airport to Cairo, Colin was put on a stretcher, even though he was perfectly able to sit up. That way it was possible for the aircraft to accommodate as many patients on stretchers in three tiers, supported on brackets, as passengers sitting on the longitudinal benches along opposite walls like parachutists:

With the engines off while we waited for take-off, there was no air cooling or ventilation and it was baking hot. Then we endured a six-hour flight towards Cairo. It was very late in the day and I got hungrier and hungrier, having had nothing since 5a.m. In due course, we landed and driven to the 15th Scottish General Hospital on the banks of the Nile. It was there that I managed to eat two dinners!

By now the skin of Colin's wound had healed but it was only skin over a reasonably-sized hole in his skull. Eventually, if no tumours grew in the ensuing months, he would need a bone graft. He remained at the 15th Scottish General Hospital for about four weeks for observation and healing. During Colin's short stay there he received an aerogram from his friend Ken Bartlett, dated 28 August 1943, written from 3 Troop headquarters at Eastbourne in England. In it Ken wrote:

My dear Colin, We were all very sorry to hear of your bad luck but are glad that you seem to be getting on alright. We envy you (not only because of oranges and ice-cream). As you see we are still in Eastbourne ... I am sharing my billets with Ernest now, a most agreeable partnership. My oboe is doing very badly; I hardly ever play. But I still play quartet & enjoy it tremendously. I hope I'll hear from you directly one of these days & hope that it will be good news. All the very best, ever yours Kenneth.

Ernest had added at the bottom:

Get well quickly and keep out of further trouble! Cracks in the skull seem to become quite fashionable. Keep the flag flying and better luck for the future. Looking forward to seeing you in Berlin.

The latter comment expressed the sentiments of many in 3 Troop that, after their respective actions, they would meet in Berlin, knowing that the Allied forces were ultimately heading for the invasion of Germany. Whilst at the 15th Scottish General, Colin was able to help on the wards, but an incident reminded him of the wound to his head:

Being an up-patient I helped with routine tasks, such as fetching meals for the ward. On one occasion, the lift stopped an inch or two below floor level, and as I lifted the front of the dinner trolley over the resulting step there was a crash behind me. My colleague dropped his end on seeing the skin covering the hole in my head balloon out from the slight effort of me lifting the trolley, from its usual concave aspect.

At the beginning of September 1943, Colin was granted a week's leave on a houseboat moored not far from the hospital on the opposite bank. It was a wonderfully luxurious holiday with a small cabin to himself, good meals and leisure time to look around Cairo. It was then that he got to know the 'Music for All' club in the city:

It was well equipped with a concert hall for recitals and music lectures; also a café for coffee and cakes, a masseur and hairdressers. It was really a great place to visit. Of importance was that as you passed through its doors, you left your jacket and any badges of rank there. Therefore you never knew who you were talking to because we had left our ranks in the army or air force as we came in. You might be talking to a colonel or a private. It didn't matter.

From the 15th Scottish General Hospital Colin was transferred to the Infantry Reinforcement Training Depot at Geneifa on the banks of the Great Bitter Lake, part of the Suez Canal. There he spent three tedious months and was downgraded to B3 which meant he was nowhere near fit enough to be a soldier, let alone a commando. It was an absolutely soul-destroying time:

It was nothing but sand, tents and bugles from morning to night. The personnel were strict. I would rather have been sent to the front than stay in that awful camp. I got to the stage where I began to deteriorate mentally because of the boredom and lack of any future. I lost the incentive to read or do anything. I became a post orderly, a terribly boring job and got more and more depressed because I could see myself ending the war in that position. It was all very disheartening.

It was in this camp that Colin fell victim to a bout of 'gyppie tummy'. As a result of the time spent in the latrine, he had to choose between two options: either to shave and miss parade, or attend parade unshaven. Either attracted penalties. He decided that attending parade unshaven was the lesser offence and might not even be noticed. But it was, and he was put on a charge. He was to report to the orderly room at eight o'clock the following morning:

The next day I tried to explain, but the arrogant young lieutenant cut me short: 'sheer bloody –idleness eight days' CB, dismiss. 'Eight days' 'jankers' was quite lenient really, and 'confined to barracks' in the literal sense quite meaningless as there was nowhere to go anyway. But it entailed various impositions to drive the point home. One was 'fatigues' like cookhouse duties and other labours, doing which I spent happy, contemplative hours peeling potatoes in conversation with other sufferers. I had to attend 'defaulter's parades'. The evening one involved the NAAFI manager being led round our ranks by a sergeant major with a pressure lamp, illuminating our faces so he should recognise any of us trying to enter the canteen from which we were banned while under punishment. It all felt a bit medieval, and almost romantic as a relic of the historic past of empire.

On 5 October 1943, Ken Bartlett penned an air letter to him addressed to the camp in the hope of raising his spirits. Already Colin had aspirations to re-join his unit after recovery. At times it looked doubtful, as indicated by Ken in his air letter:

> I saw the Skipper [Brian Hilton-Jones] about you this morning. He was very sympathetic & said he would try his damnedest to get you back to the Troop. We need a few men to do certain things here, even if you are not quite fit; there is a lot you can do. He is getting in touch with Combined Ops directly. Don't take it for granted that you will come back but you can be assured that everything possible will be done this end... I was very glad to hear that you are making good progress & hope to have some news from you directly.

Amidst the gloomy and demoralising time in the Infantry Reinforcement Training Depot, Colin had what he describes as a 'man Friday moment':

> One day I saw in the sand the impression of a SV sole that was the special rubber-like moulded sole which were issued to the commandos.[26] Only we had them at this time on our army boots. I saw the imprint of somebody who must be one of my brothers in the commandos. I tracked this footprint which led me to a tent. Inside was Mac Franklin who was a good friend from 3 Troop. He had been wounded in action in Sicily and was in this camp. We became really good friends and spent our days together. We went to Cairo together when we could get a pass. One day, we got a lift on an open truck, and I remember standing behind the cab and leaning my elbows on its roof, enjoying the ride towards Cairo. Suddenly, I began to feel quite ill, my mouth was hot and my tongue felt swollen and bone-dry: the hot, dry airflow over the speeding vehicle had dehydrated me. When I sat down in the shelter of the cab I felt better, but the real cure came in Cairo, at Groppy's, a favourite café. Their excellent Turkish coffee was a treat, but the best thing was the glass of clear, ice-cold water that came with it!
>
> Mac moved heaven and earth to get back to his troop because he wanted to take part in D-Day when it came. I was now fond of the marines too and wanted to return to them. We discussed how we could get back to our units. That boosted our morale. In due course, both our wishes were fulfilled. I was deeply shocked to learn later that Mac was killed on D-Day whilst landing on the beach. I, on the other hand, did not have another serious scratch for the whole of the war. It was very hard to come to terms with the loss of comrades in action. It was always expected, but it doesn't make it any easier to cope with.

During the waiting period at the Infantry Reinforcement Training Depot, Colin had privilege leave which he chose to spend in Palestine. Just before he left, there was a fair in the camp and he won the Bren gun firing competition. With the prize money, he purchased a suitcase.

Colin travelled by train across the Sinai desert. He had been given two addresses from fellow patients whilst he had been in hospital. He took the opportunity to call on these contacts, one in Haifa, the other in Jerusalem. Haifa did not leave much of an impression on him and from there he travelled to Tel Aviv which at that time he found shabby and noisy. Whilst in Tel Aviv, he ran into another ex-refugee from 87 Company Pioneer Corps who was also in special forces. That former comrade was walking through Tel Aviv with another soldier and introduced Colin as Mr Anzone [sic]. 'We were so used to being security conscious,' says Colin, 'that he was careful not to mention my original name.' From there, Colin went to Jerusalem where he was able to visit the biblical sites so familiar from his Protestant upbringing:

> I fell in love with Jerusalem and the old city. I had been given the address of the Moller family who lived in Rehavia, a quarter of the city that was rather European. They were quite well off. It had leafy boulevards, with houses that reminded me so much of affluent Berlin. The inhabitants in this quarter spoke German, even the children, until one of their school friends appeared and they would lapse into Ivrit (modern Hebrew). This family had a daughter Ruth, with whom I promptly fell in love. During the two weeks that I was there, we went out and about together. It was a moving and exciting time. We attended concerts at the university. One of the lasting memories is of listening to Schubert's Unfinished Symphony. Even now, I can not listen to that piece without seeing Ruth's face before me. Time seemed to stand still whilst I was there, almost like an eternity. It contained a life-time of impressions. In particular I found it very emotional to be in Jerusalem, to stand and look across the valley to the Mount of Olives and see sites which had meant a great deal during my religious instruction as a German schoolboy.

The trip to Palestine was soon at an end and Colin began the journey by train back across the desert to Geneifa. It afforded him the opportunity to look around Ismailia:

> The place was very French in character. In the station square there were dignified men in open air cafes sucking on their hubble-bubbles. I sampled the Turkish coffee before eventually making my way back to Geneifa. The whole area was one succession of camps at the time, especially POW camps. The

POW camps were enclosed with barbed wire and intensive lights all around them. The night air of the area around the canal was glimmering with all these lights. It was surreal in a way because I was so used to the black-out in the war. Our camp did not have a proper railway station; it was more of a halt without platforms. From the high train we had to jump down onto the sandy ground. Jumping from the train, I landed with a jolt. I discovered that I was left with the handle of the little suitcase I had bought for the journey in my hand. The handle had parted company with the case itself, revealing it to be made of cardboard with a thin veneer of leather. But it had served its purpose and lasted just long enough.

In December 1943 Colin was sent back to the 15th Scottish General Hospital in Cairo for a bone graft to close over the hole in his skull. The medical team had to ensure that there were no tumours or infections on the brain so it would be safe to carry out the graft. Colin underwent extensive tests to monitor the condition of his brain and central nervous system which included lumbar punctures, efficiently performed by the well-practiced nurses:

I had to lie on my side and draw up my knees as high as possible, while they inserted a syringe between the vertebrae to withdraw spinal fluid to be tested. Care was needed to avoid damage to the spinal cord. And finally before the operation, there was an X-ray encephalogram to check the condition of the brain. This was rather more of a procedure than the electro encephalograms (EEG) nowadays, and involved the fluid in which the brain is suspended being drained, so that the brain is unsupported and any growths or irregularities would bulge out, to be seen in the x-ray being taken immediately afterwards. I had a severe headache for three days afterwards while the fluid reconstituted itself.

Colin's condition was declared safe enough for a bone graft operation. The bone had to come from someone else. He asked the surgeon Captain Fraser on his daily round how long he might have to wait for the operation. His eyes scanned the heads of some very ill patients and then glanced back to Colin's, as though assessing which would be a good fit. Then said: 'oh, two or three days, two or three days…' It was just before Christmas that he had the bone he needed:

The medical orderly who shaved my head told me afterwards that he had the requisite piece of bone in his pocket, but did not feel it would have been a good idea to show it to me. The operation was a complete success, and the atmosphere in the ward became quite Christmassy as the nurses stuck bunches of cotton wool on the windows to simulate snow, and the kind ladies of the English Colony came to visit and bring gifts of chocolate, cakes and cigarettes to 'our poor dear boys'. While I was at this hospital, a soldier was admitted who had dived into the Nile to save a little Egyptian girl who fell in from one of the dhows – and as a reward he spent a week there undergoing a course of painful injections to protect him from the multiple infections rife in the river, which is the main drain and sewer of north-west Africa.

Colin had been out of action for nearly six months. As he gradually recovered, he was able to go on army leave and take a trip into Cairo where he visited the 'Music for All' club, which he had grown to love:

> On one occasion there, I had a strange co-incidence when I met another ex-refugee from 87 Company Pioneer Corps. At the back of the main building was an open space with comfortable rattan chairs. As I passed them there was an old comrade by the name of Ulanowski. Aware of the tact we employed before calling people by their names, I occupied a chair next to him. He was a brilliant pianist and had been part of the orchestra of 87 Company. He was now in SOE and had taken part in some secret operations but was a little disillusioned by it. I asked if he could help with my transfer to something more useful because until now I had not achieved anything except being highly trained, sent out to action and wounded. 'No, no', he replied, 'you are doing better where you are. Stay put.' But my ultimate aim was still to return to my unit. I was increasingly restless for frontline action, for which I had been physically and psychologically trained.

On 11 January 1944, Ken Bartlett wrote to Colin at the 15th Scottish General Hospital. Whether or not Colin would be able to return to his unit was still a matter of doubt:

> Wire to me as soon as you are discharged from hospital, giving me your address where you are going to & your medical category, if you have had your board. We'll apply for your posting immediately after arrival of your wire.

After the bone graft at the 15th Scottish General, Colin was transferred to a convalescence camp at Alexandria. Unfortunately the weather was terrible because it was now mid-January 1944:

> The camp itself was excellent, located on the beach outside Alexandria with excellent facilities but the weather was too bad to use them. There was a very welcoming Jewish Forces Club, staffed by volunteers from the Jewish

community. It was here that sumptuous meals and buffet of half chicken could be enjoyed.

Colin was determined to return to the Royal Marine Commandos and eventually succeeded. From Alexandria he was sent to a transit camp, Abbassia barracks, south of Cairo to await posting. When he arrived he discovered it to be an old-fashioned colonial British army complex, with the usual array of buildings, the NAAFI and a church. He was billeted in two-storey barracks which had a roof veranda. He recalls:

The sleeping arrangements were primitive; sleeping on the floor, not in beds, was the norm. I quickly learned how to make a very comfortable bed out of three blankets as a cocoon for myself. After the inoculations, which were regular in the army, it was usual to react to them and have a temperature. I remember one time after a vaccination, having a temperature and waking up on the opposite side of the room, but my little cocoon was still intact! Another night, I made my cocoon on the concrete floor, stretched out and thought 'Oh, how very comfortable and soft.' Then I reprimanded myself – you idiot. You're lying on a concrete floor, which is anything but soft! But in contrast to the knobbly roots of olive trees of Sicily or the uneven and stony sand of the desert surface of Geneifa, it felt very comfortable.

If I had any money whilst at this transit camp, I went into Cairo. Money was an unpredictable factor because sometimes the pay caught up with us, but often the logistics of the Pay Corps had not caught up with the new posting. The facilities at Abbassia barracks were fine, as long as you understood that the one thing you don't do is to report to that first parade which everybody has to attend. Then for the purpose of routine parades you don't exist. You could still queue up for breakfast and lunch, etc, but people don't bother you. We spent time in the NAAFI drinking 'kazoos', a lemonade-type drink, and watching the kite hawks that tended to swoop down and snatch your pretzel. It was a pleasant, but slightly boring time. The company was good and I made friends with the organist of the church there.

In due course, and declared fit for commando duties, Colin left Abbassia and was on his way back to 40 Commando in Italy. The unit was now part of No. 2 Central Mediterranean Commando Brigade which consisted two army commandos and two Royal Marine commandos. Once he returned to Italy, the 'Nobby Legends' of comrade Nobby Kendal continued to circulate, this time from the period when Colin had been recovering in hospital:

During the period when I was wounded and in hospital, Nobby was in Italy on active commando fighting. One day he was on patrol on the Garigliano where they patrolled on the other side of the river during a more static phase of the Italian campaign during the winter of 1943–44. He approached a German pillbox and instead of saying 'unless you are out of there in 20 seconds, there's a pole-charge coming through your firing slot', he gave a reasoned lawyer's dissertation as to why it would be wise for them to come out. There was a deadly silence whilst they listened. When he had finished, there was a roar of laughter and they started firing again. Nobby had his way!

In February 1944 the battle of Monte Ornito was a very hard-fought action, during which the peak was taken, then re-taken by a German counter-attack, and finally taken again and then held. Throughout this fierce battle, Nobby Kendal had carried a basket of homing pigeons which could be used for sending messages if other communications broke down; radio reception was unreliable in mountainous country. The basket was secured by the carrying handle protruding through a slot in the lid. When the battle was finally ended with the British in possession of the mountain peak, Nobby sat down and pulled out his handkerchief to wipe the sweat off his bald head. As he put down the basket, he let go of the handle, the lid opened and the pigeons flew home.

The Nobby Legends were not the only news to catch up with Colin on his return to Italy. He was more than ready for action and raids behind enemy lines, but that euphoria was tinged with sadness and the news that some of his comrades had died in the fighting or were missing in action:

Our commander Captain Ephraims of A Troop 40 Commando had been killed at Termoli. During my period out of action, my comrades had been involved in some of the liveliest actions: included Monte Cassino (where our Polish troop distinguished itself), Anzio, Salerno, Monte Ornito, the Garigliano river (where Brian Grant lost part of his leg), and the bitter winter of 43–44 in the southern Apennines. My comrade Hugh Miles from 3 Troop, with whom I had first gone out to Sicily, lived through the action at Termoli. We all knew the risks. Because of the nature of our unit and operations, none of us really expected to survive the war. We could not sit back and let someone else fight this war. It was my duty to return to my unit as soon as fit enough and get on with the job in hand.

CHAPTER 7

Commando Raids

I n the spring of 1944 Colin was on his way back to Italy to join his comrades, now attached to No 2. Commando Brigade, Central Mediterranean Force under the command of Brigadier Tom Churchill. Colin was to serve as a member of the Intelligence Section along with comrades Hugh Miles and 'Nobby' George Kendall (Knobloch); the section headed by Captain Jupp. Colin landed at Taranto, in the 'instep' of the Italian boot, after a very stormy journey from Alexandria:

> The Mediterranean can get very violent, very quickly, and every time the ship was pitching it was possible to hear the screws racing until the stern pitched down and dipped them under water so they resumed their normal rate of revolution. There was a Polish unit on board, and it was rumoured that they had a bear with them who was their mascot. Our hearts went out to the poor animal which was probably unused to travelling at sea in heavy weather.

They landed in Southern Italy amidst air raid warnings and a place shrouded in smoke screen. From there he took a slow train up towards Naples:

> It was all excitement because we got to Naples when there was an eruption of Vesuvius. We were not allowed to leave the train, which waited in a siding outside Naples. I craned my neck out of the door, but couldn't actually see the volcano. Eventually we were back on track and I was able to reach the transit camp where I was heading.

Colin waited in the tented transit camp, inland from Naples. It was a terrible camp and the weather was awful. The tents had tears in them and were not really waterproof. The food was dreadful and had undesirable results on the digestive system:

> Most of us suffered the effects of the food, woken in the night half conscious; knowing that unless I got up to the toilet, I would have an accident. I stumbled in the dark through the tents and mud, falling over ropes, to finally reach a latrine, only to join the end of a lengthy queue, with figures holding their stomachs and groaning to themselves.
>
> Whilst we were in the camp we went a couple of times into Naples to present arms while the flags were being run up the flagpoles for an Allied conference. We had to supply the personnel for parades which were filmed in the central boulevard through Naples. There were lots of flagpoles along the boulevard. We were required to present arms and then filmed. The film crew would stop us and we would have to do it all over again. At this time we were also taken out in lorries on working parties which proved a welcome relief from the monotony of the camp.

This period had other memorable incidents for Colin too, like the occasion when there were no Italian personnel working in the munitions dumps due to the Easter holidays. Colin and his comrades found themselves sorting and loading ammunition. On their way back to camp, their lorry got hopelessly stuck in a large crowd in front of the town hall of a small village:

> It was quite a sight with large tapestries draped over the balcony of the first floor of the Town Hall. The mayor and priests were out as part of the festivities. We could do nothing except watch because we couldn't move our vehicle through the crowd. After the litany and final prayers everyone suddenly opened their mouths and chanted in unison, 'Amen'. And the whole place was filled with an intense odour of garlic. It was one of those bizarre incidents I have never forgotten.

Eventually, the men were able to return to the transit camp. Colin was eventually informed of his next posting and was to make his way to his unit at Monopoli on the east side of southern Italy. No sooner had he arrived than he was moved immediately to the Adriatic island of Vis, off the coast of Yugoslavia, the base for the Commando Brigade. That became their base for the summer of 1944 from where they were to raid the German island garrisons in the Adriatic. On landing in Vis, they moved inland and settled in the main valley above Komiža, the harbour town at the West of the island:

That summer was idyllic. We all fell in love with the island. There were no facilities as such, but it was summertime. In our spare time we were able to go swimming and other activities. The main purpose of my work was to interrogate prisoners. I acted as the German speaker/translator on motor gunboat patrols along the coast. I was to shout the captain's orders to the German crew of any craft in the seas, but we didn't actually intercept any German boats at that time. Whilst fellow commando Nobby and I were sharing a tent on Vis, living in the valley above Komiža, Captain Jupp established the intelligence section in a small farmhouse. Nobby and I knew each other very well, although we were not intimate friends. During action, he would never lead his section when we were advancing behind another one, but went right through the field of fire of the section that was covering him. It was later during one of our raids that we came under artillery fire. An experienced ear could notice that it wasn't coming towards us but going over somewhere else. We were with a group of young marines who were not yet battle-hardened like us. Everyone went flat on their faces. Suddenly Nobby and I were the only ones standing up! We smiled at each other.

During Colin's time on Vis there was quite a lot of air activity. In the valley there was a small airstrip which was the only place for aircraft to land on the island:

We were at first briefly near Vis, the main town of the island. At the 'English Cemetery', near Fort George which housed a British garrison during the Napoleonic wars, I smoked a cigarette while sitting on the gravestone of a naval officer called Anson! It was from a hillside above the airstrip in one of the two small valleys in the interior of the island, this one nearer the town of Vis, that we witnessed the aircraft on the proper approach which was recognised as a German plane only after they had fired at the landing area and dropped bombs. Later the arrival of a Macchi fighter approaching from the wrong direction and height which was fired at before it landed and turned out to be Italian, now on our side. It had hardly come to a stop before the canopy flew back and the pilot, standing up in the cockpit, gave a most expressive display of furiously indignant gesturing.

On one occasion we saw an incoming twin-boomed fighter, a P38 Lockheed 'Lightning', aircraft which had been damaged and could not make it back across the Adriatic. It put down, but the airstrip was very short. It tried to stop at the end of the runway and couldn't, only to disappear down a ravine. We thought that was it. No one could survive that and we sent a jeep out to get the body, whereupon the canopy slid back and the RAF pilot undid himself and stood up. He simply said, 'Oh, thanks very much chaps.' He hopped out and then added:

'Just a minute. I haven't switched off the guns'. But the guns were in the nose of the fuselage and no longer capable of firing. His reaction and comment was quite comical in a way. Other air activity came from bombers and C47s. There were quite a number of them. They had been on bombing missions to target Romanian oil. One of the planes had been shot up, couldn't make it back across the Adriatic, so circled Vis for a time on autopilot. Eventually we counted the parachutes that came out of it and the men were subsequently rescued from the sea. The aircraft eventually went into the side of a mountain in the valley beyond the airstrip.

Meanwhile back in Britain, the final operations and manoeuvres were being put into place for D-Day and the invasion of Normandy. 'For us on Vis at this time,' comments Colin, 'it was not all combat dramatics. There were quiet periods.' On odd occasions, his bone graft gave him cause for concern:

When I rested or slept in my tent, I tended to lie with my head on my right palm. One evening I suddenly found that the fingers of my right hand were pressing against something that was giving way. I instantly thought my bone graft was coming loose, so next morning I reported to the first aid post. The doctor started pushing and knocking the skull. Apparently it was all fine. It had come a bit loose because the sutures which held the graft in place until it had bedded in with the surrounding skull had dissolved. The surrounding skull grows towards it and overlaps and underlaps it. That eventually became stronger than the original.

Then came the commando raids on the German garrisons on the islands of Brač and Hvar. From their base in Vis, the men were sent out on these night raids. The most spectacular raid in which Colin took part was on the island of Brač on 2–4 June 1944. It was arranged rather hurriedly in the light of German and partisan activities, at the time when Marshal Tito was nearly captured by the Germans in the cave complex near Drvar which was the partisan headquarters. At the time of the German attack, Randolph Churchill and Evelyn Waugh were with Tito as Allied representatives.

Our landing was harmless but rather messy. It was early morning but still dark. We went, not in assault craft, but in LSI (Landing Ship Infantry), a rather larger vessel. We were a bit crowded and had a number of partisans on board. Once we had come close to the beach, the ramps of our vessel went down, but were found not to be long enough. So doors were unhinged from the officer's mess and used. We were waiting to get off and it was an uncomfortable time because we could be vulnerable to opposing fire. But fortunately nothing happened. Then we tried to get off the vessel, but couldn't because the partisans were sitting on our stores. So the partisans landed first, distributed themselves about the beach and much to our horror started lighting cigarettes. This was not a good start because it could have alerted the Germans to our landing. Then the Royal Marines and Army Commandos (Nos. 43 and 40) finally got off and we started trudging inland and uphill. We found afterwards that the landing was being watched by a German observation post in the mountainside above the beach, whose machine guns could have wiped us out – but they thought it wiser just to observe, and were then taken prisoner.

I was carrying a sack full of tins as our food supplies, which was often heavy going. Brač is a very mountainous island and tough terrain when on foot. We arrived at a small hamlet of a few houses in the hamlet of Obersje. An older couple gave us water for our flasks. We heard a rumour later that the couple was thrown into the flames of their burning cottage as a punishment for having helped us. It was during this action that we saw German aircraft for the last time in the air during daytime. Two German fighters were flying along the coast, towards our landing beach, probably intending to attack our LSI. Two Hurricanes appeared behind them, as though they had been lying in wait behind a mountain to ambush them and shot both the German fighters down.

Eventually the group settled on a hilltop in the middle of the island. The following day they observed an American carpet-bombing raid going on over Split. They had a full view of the air raid: 'It looked as if the whole town was going to be obliterated. There was lots of smoke and dust but we found out later that it had hardly been touched. The place largely consisted of ancient imperial ruins.'

A few days later, the commando group radioed for RAF for help in attacking German positions on a neighbouring hilltop which was well-fortified. A 'circus' was sent out, i.e. hurricanes which circled above and waited for orders from the ground. They had with them an RAF controller who erected his aerial and wireless, then started to take up contact with the aircraft overhead. From the ground came orders for the heavily defended German position on a neighbouring hilltop to be targeted:

The next thing we knew was the area around us was crackling with shells and machine gun bullets. The controller controlled the canon shell through his own wireless mast, which caused the air to go extremely blue when he was talking on his radio. It was extremely noisy, but nobody amongst us got hit. It made it plain to me how chancy these things are. Even in the most dramatic circumstances, nothing may happen, or in the most harmless circumstances, things may go disastrously wrong.

One of the reasons for being on Brač was to raise as much noise and dust as possible to make it sound like a big operation. The aim was to draw German troops towards *them* and away from their hunt for Tito, the leader of the partisans:

> We were opposed by the SS Division *Prinz Eugen*, largely made up of Balkan personnel, local Yugoslav fascists and Austrian Nazi officers. They were a highly unpleasant group of individuals. We spun it out until we were sure that it had had some effect. We sat on the mountain tops with SS panzers heading for us, a particularly hazardous time for us. It was uncomfortable to find the masked-headlights of the SS Division coming closer and closer. Yet the strategy was highly successful because it enabled Tito and his partisans to escape through the back of the cave where he was hiding. Tito spent some time on the island of Vis under heavy Allied military protection, then the rest of the war on the mainland with partisan forces.

Often with little sleep whilst on missions in enemy territory, Colin took the opportunity to rest:

> One afternoon after a small recce mission that Captain Jupp had sent me out on, I went to sleep. A while later, I woke. The soles of both of my feet were in acute pain because the sun had moved around behind the rock where I had bedded down. The bottom of my feet with their rubber soles on my boots had been exposed to the full blast of the afternoon sun. That made my feet pretty hot!
>
> On another occasion, I was sent out on a mission to find out if there were any German units which were supposed to have settled some miles away. I went up hill and down, arrived at where I was supposed to go but there was no sign of anyone there or having been there. So I made my way back which took quite a while. On the way I fell in with an American who was walking the same way. I had no idea who he was or what he was doing there. Unlike me, he had a Tommy gun with a magazine of thirty rounds. I envied that, so he said: 'Oh, we'll swap'. I gave him my magazine in exchange for his. We parted company. I found out afterwards why he wasn't bothered about parting with his thirty-round magazine because the damn thing kept falling off. I had to file a little nick into the magazine retaining catch to stop it falling off.

Whilst Colin was on Brač, there was an incident with 'Mad Jack' Churchill of 2 Commando Brigade who was taken prisoner:

During attacks on German hilltop positions, due to an unfortunate communications mix-up, there were heavy casualties, Col. 'Pop' Manners of 40 Commando was mortally wounded, and Colonel 'Mad Jack' Churchill of 2 Commando Briagde was taken prisoner. He had his bagpipes with him, kilt and sword and had been playing: *Will ye not come back again*. It was suggested that I was sent behind the lines to rescue him, but I did not think it a wise mission without any proper preparation. It would have been totally foolhardy to mount unplanned rescue because an important prisoner like him would hardly have been kept on the island, but would have been immediately sent to the mainland. He was in fact immediately flown to Germany. After escaping from Sachsenhausen concentration camp he walked all the way to the Baltic, to be recaptured a few miles from the shore, and finally escaped from a camp in the Tyrol to walk 150 miles to Verona where he contacted an American column. Of my own contact with Colonel Churchill I particularly remember a time when I returned from leave in Italy by a ship which Churchill met at Komiža to collect some goods he had ordered. He gave me a lift to the location of the intelligence section in his open jeep, skidding round the hairpins of the gravel road up from the coast and scaring the daylights out of me. I last saw him at the pub in the Strand which served as the commando rendezvous, where he and his brother (now General) Tom invited me to have drinks with them, and we sang such partisan songs as we remembered.

There was one mission where 212 Battery of 111 Field Regiment RA, landing 25-pounder guns, took precise measurements on aerial photographs, planned the operation very precisely and had themselves landed on the shore of a neighbouring island, opposite where the Germans were. They spent the rest of the night laying their guns because they did not want to give away their presence by firing ranging shots. They meticulously adjusted their guns as best they could. In the morning when the Germans were all queuing up for breakfast with their mess tins, they put down a barrage of rapid fire and before the dust had completely settled and the Germans had recovered from the unpleasant surprise, they were back on their landing craft and on their way. This was typical of the unusual schemes dreamed up by various units during our pirates' existence in the region.

There was another occasion when the Royal Navy did the same. Two motor gun boats were taken out, carefully camouflaging themselves against the shore of one of the fjords along the rocky coast of that part of Yugoslavia. They waited until one of the convoys came along which was taking provisions to the German garrisons. And when they were broadside on, they opened up and raked their decks, at the same time starting their engines. By the time the escorts had woken up and had begun turning their guns around, the raider had sped out in the opposite direction and came back along the other side and raked their decks again. At this time unlikely units, like the Royal Navy, performed improbable raids on their own. We sometimes went with them as boarding parties and interpreters.

Colin went out twice on coastal patrols in a motor torpedo boat. It was here that his knowledge of German would be used if needed. If they came across a German vessel, he was to shout with a loud speaker in German: 'We're British, stop! Otherwise you will be torpedoed.' It was very important to declare that they were British because the Germans hated the possibility of being taken by partisans, from whom they did not expect fair treatment. It was on one of these coastal patrols that Colin learnt something about Naval slang:

> A kindly Naval Officer explained to me the meaning of the epithet 'Pongo' by which sailors and airmen nickname their foot-slogging army brothers-in-arms. I always wondered what that meant because we had heard the term used of us. He explained to me that a pongo is a small mud-coloured furry animal of low intelligence which crawls along the ground in southern America. That was why they called us pongos. But, I was an army commando soldier attached to the Royal Marine Commandos, and granted the honour of being promoted to the rank, style and title of 'Ma-Pong' which meant half-marine, half-pongo! We all got on very well and as such I was considered half a marine!

Then came 6 June 1944: on the other side of Europe, the flag went up for D-Day – the massive Allied invasion of Normandy. The Allied forces were to see fierce fighting in the orchards and hedgerows of northern France and especially in the advance on Caen through the bocage. Some of Colin's comrades from 3 Troop were attached to units for spearheading the advance through Normandy towards Belgium and eventually into Germany. At this time Colin was still involved in raids on the Yugoslav islands, little knowing just how severe the casualties and fatalities would be for 3 Troop.[27] Colin comments:

> We heard about the D-Day landings because we were quite well informed and had radios. But what I did not know was the fate of some of my comrades from 3 Troop. On one occasion, the RAF dropped us newspapers with the latest developments about the liberation of Paris on 25 August 1944. We drank Rakia

to celebrate the occasion. It was the yellow Rakia which can be quite vicious and make you feel your head is going to explode. It was important to celebrate this – we had been through so much up to that point.

After action lasting only a few days, the commando raiders left Brač and returned to their base in Vis. As they left, this time aboard a landing craft tank (LCT), they were in the company of partisans: 'Partisan girls were singing folk songs in long drawn out voices. It was evening, and with the calm sea as we were drawing closer to Vis, it was all terribly romantic.' Colin carried out routine intelligence activities with his unit. There were extra curricular activities such as the production of a daily magazine called *The Daily Vis-à-Vis* which gave news items, some of which came from the partisans with whom they came into contact. On Sundays there was a bumper issue called *The Vis of the World*. Both provided soldiers on Vis with an up-to-date report of Allied progress in France, Italy, Russia and the Balkans. On 23 August 1944 the hundredth issue came out. The editor proudly wrote:

It fills us with great pleasure that what was started in an idle moment has become an institution in the garrison which most of its members have got used to. We have tried in the past to uphold as far as possible in wartime, the principle of liberty of thought and freedom of the press ... The success is, however, mainly due to a most loyal staff who did all the work on top of their daily routine.

Colin was one of the members of staff engaged in the printing of these newspapers when he was not on raids on the other islands. *The Daily Vis-à-Vis* and *The Vis of the World* were both published by the intelligence section of No.2 Commando Brigade, with whom Colin was engaged. He recalls:

I acted as the 'printer', typed the articles on to wax stencils on which I also traced the illustrations, pricking them through the wax coating with a pin, and rolled them off on a *Gestetner* duplicator which, in these dusty condition, needed a certain amount of maintenance. I also contributed a daily news column. And I was in charge of our store of maps of the Dalmatian coast and islands, as far south as Albania. I was astonished to find that many were issued by the British Ordnance Survey, and with their excellent quality.

Activities in Yugoslavia were increasingly dominated by the partisans themselves. In September 1944, 2 Commando Brigade left the Yugoslav island of Vis. Nobby Kendal returned to Italy and was attached to a specialist interrogation unit based in Naples. It was there that he fulfilled an important role because, with his legal mind, he was a first rate interrogator. He was assigned to particular cases dealing with Germans who had specialist knowledge and who had to be interrogated with great care: 'He could completely demolish their arguments,' adds Colin, 'until they became so exasperated that they blurted out everything he needed to know.' A small group, including Colin, remained for a short time on Vis: 'cleaning up various things. Then eventually we sailed back to Italy in a Caique, a round-bellied sailing ship which can get close in to the rocky Adriatic shores, used as fishing or trading vessels in the Mediterranean. We had a very agreeable sea journey back to Italy.'

Having served a little longer on Vis than other colleagues, the detachment which included Colin finally returned to Italy. It was now late summer of 1944 and the men were quartered in Monopoli. They were about to be dispatched for their next mission: landing in Albania. From Monopoli they travelled to Rimini, embarking for Albania at the naval base of Brindisi on the south-east coast for what was supposed to be a short, sharp action. In the end it lasted from around 22 September until 21 October:

> We went down to Brindisi and crossed the Adriatic to a place close to the southern end of Albania. It was there that we carried out a landing in a small bay north of Sarande. It was still quite warm and we were in tropical kit. Once we had landed, we dug in but were within artillery range of the north end of the Greek island of Corfu. The Germans were well ensconced there and showered us with shrapnel from their 88mm guns from the northern tip of Corfu.

They advanced through ravines towards the ridge overlooking a plain beyond, at the other end of which is the Albanian town Argirocastro (now Gjirokaster). They did not get far because the weather broke. The intention was to take the southern Albanian port of Sarande but all operations were delayed for three weeks because of the heavy rains which engulfed everything:

> The rain came down with a vengeance. It was like being in a cold monsoon of incessant heavy rain. We put on our anti-gas capes. I always remember the sight of a little clearing in the undergrowth where we were advancing, with the sight of lots of little pyramids, that being our men sat on their packs with gas capes over their heads, looking out through the ventilation holes in the armpits. The situation became rather static because we couldn't move.

The men were not in tents, not during action. They lived in the coastal hills with very little shelter and under occasional artillery fire from the well dug-in Germans. Colin dug himself a slit trench under a rock face: 'It wasn't comfortable,' he comments, 'because we were wet through twenty-four hours a day.'

Whenever I had time off and wanted to go to bed, I would kneel on the edge of the slit trench and fish in the bottom of it until I found some resistance, then pulled out my blanket. It was dripping wet and immersed in mud. I did 'go to bed', not undressing, wrapping the blanket around me and using my steel helmet as a pillow because that was the only thing that wasn't wet through. I stayed very still all night and that way it was possible to warm up those bits of uniform that were touching my skin. The trick was not to move and lose contact with the warmed-up bit of wet uniform. I also had a ground sheet wedged into the little cracks in that rock by bits of twig such that it sloped across my trench. I was under primitive cover at least. I even had a book to read, even though it was soaked through! I had a candle which I wedged, so I could read by the light of it! At times, there would be a small avalanche of earth from the side of my slit trench, and a goggle-eyed bug might stick its head out, perhaps attracted by the light, before retreating back into the earth wall. We were all wet for the whole three weeks, but survived. That's what we had been trained to do – survive in difficult conditions. In more exposed forward positions where our men had to keep under cover and not move about too much, because they became visible if they moved, we did have casualties from exposure. We had as many casualties from exposure as we did from battle casualties.

In spite of the heavy rain, we went out on patrols from our 'headquarters' in the ravine. Overnight, we built up a bonfire using dead wood from the area. We waited until morning when it was light enough to dare to light it because down in our ravine it would not shine enough light to attract attention. One morning Brigadier Churchill (Jack Churchill's brother) saved me from serious injury because when we finally decided it was light enough, a tin of petrol was poured over the heap of wood. We threw a match and the whole lot went up in great flames to a wave of warmth which rolled over all of us standing right around it. Everyone started steaming because their battledress was so wet. Brigadier Churchill, who was sitting in a hollow tree like an owl waiting for the weather to recover, suddenly shot out, ripped the gas cape from my shoulders and trampled on it. There were little blue flames licking around it because I had got too close to the bonfire.

The commando positions were bombarded periodically from an old Austrian howitzer which fired heavy-calibre shells on a high trajectory. 'When the shells started coming down,' comments Colin, 'it sounded like an express train.' The men took cover:

The shell buried itself in the silt at the bottom of the ravine and was quite harmless. It went off with a huge thump, throwing tons of earth into the air. It did no harm unless it was a direct hit. What was more harmful was shrapnel from the 88mm guns positioned on the tip of Corfu. Airbursts were sent over the ravines where we were located and that had an effect on the mules that we had. We took it in turns to go down to the beach where we had landed to pick up supplies that came in at night. We had large frames on which to load boxes of forty-eight-hour rations which came in from Italy. One day when 2 Commando was told to be ready to receive supplies, the ramp of the landing craft went down on the beach and out trotted a large number of mules. They were the larger Italian type mules with a black stripe along their backs, accompanied by Italian muleteers to supervise their handling and care. The party from No.2 Commando was told: 'They are yours'. We soon became fond of the mules, but they were sensitive to the bangs. A mule might only get a small nick of shrapnel, but the shock of it would make it shiver and drop dead. The terrain was also not suitable for them, because they were hurt by the thorns that grew on everything.

The men took it in turns to go down to the beach where they had first landed at night. With their carriers they were to pick up rations and other supplies. The rations were in the form of ration boxes each for twenty four men. The individual rations fitted into their mess tins. There were four different boxes labelled A, B, C or D, as Colin explains:

Box C had a roly-poly in it which I always enjoyed. There were also meat dishes. Sometimes we had self-heating soups in a tin, which as soon as we opened it, would heat itself. There was also a large tin box of army biscuits; set meals of varying quality, which included stew of some sort, and energy giving ready meals for breakfast, like porridge with sugar. We had tea and little cookers (solid fuel). There were energy-giving biscuits and sweets, as well as our ration of cigarettes. There was a supply of toilet paper which we had to bury as soon as we had used it so as not to give away our presence on the island. As well as group rations, we were given individual rations: again energy-giving food and other items similar to group rations.

It came to Colin's turn to collect the supplies form the beach one night. He had another near miss with death:

I went into my little slit trench that I had dug on the night of our landing to get some sleep before the supplies arrived. The field telephone rang and a message came through requiring me to go back up. I did that before returning for the rations. I dealt with the message and was soon back on the beach. Someone from the Signals Corps gave me a mug of tea. I was watching a small group of people digging furiously. One of them turned around and said: 'My goodness! There he is!' They were looking at me aghast. I didn't realise they were digging for me. Due to the bad weather, my slit trench had caved in whilst I was taking that message, and they thought I was still in it. They knew I had gone to sleep in it earlier and feared me dead.

On one occasion, Colin and two others were sent to a small fishing village up the coast, to collect a 'Dory', a small open boat with an engine mounted in a wooden box cover in the middle, to bring it back to their cove. They were taken in a jeep, driving along a road along the east side of the coastal range, overlooking the inland plain. This meant that it was also overlooked by the German self-propelled guns which roamed about in that plain. At intervals there were small stone memorials to mark the spot where someone may have been a victim of a winter avalanche or rock fall. The driver played a little game with the German gunners who used these memorials as aiming marks, as Colin explains:

So our driver approached one at a slow, steady speed, and then suddenly accelerated past it, leaving the German shell to explode behind us. Or he approached at high speed and then suddenly braked before reaching the memorial stone, and only go on after a shell had crashed into it. This seemed great fun, and made me wonder about the nature of courage, when I might enjoy this game which was quite dangerous. At another time I could be really frightened in situations like being bombed at night which were comparatively harmless. When we collected the Dory, we started on our journey down the coast, against a slight current, when the engine cut out. After much swinging of the crank handle it would start again and we would resume our journey, to have the engine stop again at much the same place. There was one particular light-coloured rock which we got to know quite well, where that engine would conk out every time. After drifting back quite some way, the engine would finally start and take us back to that same rock before repeating the performance. The swinging of the starting handle was hard on our hands, and dipping it in the salt water to lubricate it stung in the developing blisters. This went on for much of the night, and we smoked cigarettes hoping that any partisans on the shore would realise we were British and not fire at us. We just got into the cover of our cove before it grew light enough to expose us to the gun crews on the Corfu coast.

No.2 Commando Brigade was joined by another unit: the Raiding Support Regiment (RSR) which had heavier weapons: 3" mortars, .50 heavy machine guns and 75mm mountain howitzers which they could take apart quickly for transportation: 'There were times when the RSR had two guns facing outwards back to the beach in case of unpleasant surprises; then four guns which were facing forward towards the enemy. If they started firing rapid, it sounded like a regiment of artillery.'

Colin and his comrades came into contact with Germans. On one occasion a complete German field hospital surrendered and offered their services to the partisans. Another incident was when German soldiers came out through the barbed wire fence of their emplacements. All the while, a Nazi NCO covered the only gap in the fence with machine gun fire. They managed to get through their own lines, then through the partisan lines, to finally surrender to No.2 Brigade. These soldiers tended to be anti-Nazis who hated the war. They wanted to surrender or join the Allied forces to help as much as possible. Amongst them were some bizarre characters:

One particular man, a Social Democrat, used to cruise up and down outside Sarande in one of our small motor boats with loud speaker, telling the Nazis some home truths about themselves and their officers. It was quite comical in a way, but it had the desired effect of undermining German morale. Our forces used a number of tactics to undermine morale of the enemy. The Royal Engineers laid long lines of slow-burning fuses, off them were branches of fast-burning fuses which would set off lines of cartridges, sounding like machine guns going off rapidly. All sorts of sound effects were simulated to undermine the enemy's confidence. The same tactic was used in one area to draw the enemy's attention there, whilst something more important was being done elsewhere.

I also had two German sergeants for a short time under my charge who I did not take to very much. I went out in front on the ridge at the crest of the coastal mountain range, overlooking the plain. The minarets of Argirocastro across the plain made good artillery aiming marks. We went complete with a field telephone because our wireless communications were still not brilliant. I lent them my binoculars and they used to give me fire orders to relay to the RSR to put artillery fire down on their own lines. They hated their commanding officer and they had other grievances. They would say: 'Oh good that will make fat Captain _____ jump'. I found this attitude very unpleasant because I did not expect them to fire on their own people with relish. Many POWs came over to us voluntarily. When we came face-to-face with the enemy, they tended to be happy to come along with us. It was one of my jobs to interrogate the POWs. The characters were interesting and gave a very good idea of what we were up against. There was one particular enemy unit which was a punishment battalion that had been banished into the wilds of Albania. They tended not to be fond of their own side and were fed up with the war.

Colin has a number of vivid memories of the POWs who surrendered, some of whom became good acquaintances and were very helpful:

One POW when asked his name replied: '*Ich bin der Prinz von Wales*'. My eyebrows immediately shot up. Then he broke into a broad grin and explained that his name was Prinz, he was a confectioner and he came from Wels in upper Austria. So, we had a good laugh. He stayed with us for a while and cooked our meals until the next supply boat took him to a POW camp in Italy.

When the weather improved, No.2 Commando Brigade started its way south towards Sarande. It was during one of these patrols that Colin came across that group of partisans who invited him to share their roasted sweetcorn cobs:

I didn't speak their language and they didn't speak any of the languages that I could, so there was a lot of smiling and gestures. I recall burning my lips trying to gnaw the hot maize! After one of these excursions, I came down to the coast as it was getting dark. By the shore, I picked up a field telephone wire and wondered whether it was theirs or ours? But I decided to follow it south, when I heard a column approaching from the north – and they were talking in English. So I fell in with the rear of the column, approaching it carefully and identifying myself in case they might think I was German. When we were close to Sarande, probably a day or two later, I had to look after a group of prisoners near the shore, who were going to be taken to Italy on a landing craft after the supplies it had brought had been unloaded. Suddenly there was a bang, as someone had trodden on an S-mine. They have three little prongs almost invisibly poking out of the ground, and propel a canister full of ball bearings to about waist height where it then explodes. All the Germans hit the deck, but there were no more explosions, and no casualties near us. But a sailor unloading that landing craft, 100 meters further down on the shore, dropped dead: a ball bearing had pierced his heart.

Another POW of whom I grew very fond was a small, rather yellowish older man who was a plumber from Saxony. I can't remember his name but he hated the Nazis with a vengeance. He was in Punishment Battalion 99 because he had given a crust of bread to a French POW. And that was punishable. He had never been a real Nazi. He stayed with us for a while. He had been with the German Pioneers, who were more like our Royal Engineers, than our Pioneer Corps.

He was invaluable to the commandos because in the Punishment Battalion he was attached to the German Pioneers who had been responsible for laying the minefields for the Germans. His knowledge was crucial and it was he who helped lay white tapes through the minefields at night on the advance towards Sarande. It meant that the men could advance at night without fear of treading on mines. As a German speaker, Colin was assigned to look after him. Colin recalls:

> He was a charming man and so helpful, especially just before our attack on Sarande. We were sitting on the obverse of the hill before the attack. In the tiny valley at our feet the RSR was putting out some covering fire in preparation. If you leant back and looked straight up, you could actually see the mortar bombs, a little black point wobbling as it reached the apex of its trajectory and then it would go down. We were chatting together in German whilst all this was going on. He spoke with a strong Saxon accent and had a lot of pride in his craft and job satisfaction. And he said: 'And you know what gives the greatest pleasure? That is to equip a barracks. There are no divisions between the toilets and they stood in a straight row, like soldiers "dressed by the right" on parade. Ah, that gladdens your heart.' He came with us in action when we attacked Sarande in October 1944.

Colin came across an imposing building. He pushed in the door and went in with Tommy gun at the ready. Inside the hall was in darkness. Once his eyes adjusted, he soon realised that he was in the main hall of a bank, with polished mahogany semi-circular counter. From behind the counter, there suddenly came two hands, followed by a gentleman in a grey uniform. Colin told him to open the shutters so he could see. When there was some light in the room it became apparent that the bank had been turned into a German officers' mess. The semi-circular counter had become the bar. 'On the wall behind,' recalls Colin, 'were shelves with bottles of the most wonderful liquors and wines, and drinks from all over German occupied Europe. The marines weren't very far behind me and started coming in. I hopped behind the bar with the German man, and we gave out drinks! In spite of the consumption of alcohol no one had a hangover because of the quality of it.' By now the commandos were very hungry and tired. Colin discovered a loaf called *Kommissbrot* (German army bread), rather solid but quite good, and tinned sausage *Jagdwurst* (Hunter's sausage). He tucked in and enjoyed a good meal.

Now and then, there were bangs to be heard. The Germans had disappeared but they had not had time to take their considerable explosives store with them. They had used explosives to lay booby-traps: 'Anything that looked desirable (from a German car to a typewriter or binoculars) was booby-trapped and went up at the slightest touch. We had been warned about this in training.' The German POW who was a plumber was helping to defuse the booby-traps. There were no medical facilities for the commandos in Albania. The medical officer and his staff had to cope with injuries. They came into Colin's bank, bringing in the wounded on blankets. It was a surreal scenario:

They operated there and then in front of us. They used a pile of blankets as an operating table. The medical sergeant reverted to the old way of administering anaesthesia by spraying ether on to a handkerchief over the patient's face. When you see things like that on TV or films, I am liable to get near to fainting but when you are really in amongst it, the reality somehow doesn't affect me the same way. And there we were having *Jagdwurst* and drink whilst watching someone's leg being cut off. Presently our German POW plumber was brought in because he had been defusing one of the booby-traps for us and it had gone off. He wasn't badly hurt but the MO examined him below the knee and said 'I think you'll be fine. It certainly isn't an amputation, but the operation has to be done in Italy.' The marines had become fond of our plumber because he had helped us such a lot. They brought in cigarettes and chocolate for him and tears of emotion ran down his cheeks, he was so touched. He told us: 'You are such lovely people. Make sure you get those devils [the Nazis] and catch them for me and don't let them get away.' He was soon taken back to a field hospital in Italy.

While Colin and the marines were in the bank, others during their advance through Sarande, found one particular warehouse nearby full of explosives. A good effort was made by a staff officer of the Royal Engineers, who was attached to the brigade, to deal with it:

Before deserting the warehouse, the Germans had turned over all the shelves and stands. It was a real mess and almost impossible to sort out. One thing the Germans had done was to scatter time pencils around the place. These were small pencil-size detonators which have a firing pin. The pencil sized lead tube contained a fulminate of mercury detonator, a spring-loaded striker held back by a short length of copper wire, and a glass phial full of acid. Squeezing the soft tube crushes the glass, releasing the acid which will eat through the copper wire, when the spring drives the striker into the detonator to explode it. The time delay depends on the thickness [gauge] of the wire. It was impossible for us to even think of going through all the heaps of muddled explosives to find the time pencils. With typical German methodical mindset, the person who had scattered the pencils had put safety pins from them back into the cardboard box in which they came. They had left that carton on the windowsill just beside the door. We knew that that would have been the very last thing they did as they were leaving the premises. So we knew exactly what time the Germans had withdrawn from Sarande.

This Royal Engineers officer had a pretty good idea of when the time pencils were scattered and crushed in order to set them going. The cardboard boxes in which they came were marked with the type and time-delay. He was able to say that these will go off at X. For safety reasons everyone was withdrawn from Sarande and stationed halfway around the bay. We gave it an hour or two, settled down overlooking the harbour and town; an opportunity to have a good rest. We sat there, waiting for the detonation. Through all this I was in charge of a German warrant officer who wasn't a bad chap. Like every German soldier, he told us he had never been a Nazi. I chatted with him. The hour approached for the anticipated detonation and nothing happened. We waited another half an hour. Still nothing. Eventually we came to the conclusion that nothing was going to happen and that it had all gone wrong. Then BANG! And half of Sarande seemed to go up. That staff officer Royal Engineers saved a good few lives that day.

Sarande fell on 9 October 1944. Throughout all this action, not much was seen of the Albanian civilians or partisans. The Allies had limited contact with the partisans but Colin was less than impressed with them:

We had been used to the Tito partisans in Yugoslavia who were quite a disciplined and purposeful army. In Albania when there was action, we didn't see much of the partisans. After the action was over, they materialised from no where. They were not motivated in the same way as the Yugoslav partisans.

The tales of human encounter for the Allied forces are amongst the most memorable of this period. What were Colin's thoughts on coming into contact with German soldiers?

If the opponent is attacking you, he is the enemy and you attack in turn. As long as he is poised to attack, anything in a grey uniform is a target and you fire at it.

But taking prisoners is always better than killing for the sake of it. In fact, one has to guard against an urge to fraternise once the tension is off, and there is a sense of all of us being in the same situation together.

CHAPTER 8

The Liberation of Corfu

Whilst still in Albania, rumours circulated that there were still Germans on Corfu, so Colin and a fellow marine boarded a motor gunboat to take a look. The war was nearing its close and they inadvertently found themselves the liberators of the Greek island of Corfu. The motor gun boat entered the old harbour and Colin and his fellow marine jumped ashore. They expected the boat to tie up and wait for them, but much to their surprise the crew took off. Colin and his comrade were stranded on the island. Their presence was immediately noticed: 'we found ourselves surrounded by jubilant Greeks who hadn't seen an Allied soldier in four years. We were given a tumultuous welcome and dragged into the nearest *taverna* where the ouzo came out. That's about all I remember of that day!' The Italians, not the Germans, were the main occupying power on the island: 'The Italians did not treat the population too well and kept them short of food. The Germans were there as part of a garrison. They surrendered to us in a civilised manner. Corfu was now liberated. I often make a joke that I liberated Corfu quite by accident. Eventually part of our brigade arrived on the island.'

Colin and his comrade stayed overnight in a broken old seaman's shelter near the harbour, then moved into a three-star hotel. The Germans were very civilised about their arrival:

They did not want to start a private war. They courteously introduced themselves to us. The commander was Captain Rabe who spoke to me in accent-free German, saying: '*Mein Name ist Hauptmann Rabe, ungekrönter König von Korfu!'* meaning 'My name is Captain Rabe [Raven], uncrowned king of Corfu,' and laughed. He then introduced his lieutenants. It was all very civilised.

Arrangements were made for them to be evacuated to Italy where they would be interrogated and held in POW camps. The Germans were embarked on an LSI [Landing Ship Infantry] which has four holds. Their men occupied three of the holds, the fourth we reserved for the officers. Before it departed, I boarded and asked if everything was alright. Captain Rabe replied: 'yes, first class thank you very much.' I replied, 'Bon Voyage,' and then they were gone. The soldiers that were subsequently left on Corfu were an extremely sorry bunch. We housed them in the seamen's shelters by the harbour. The remaining soldiers were a detachment of Italians.

Two German soldiers Robert Neher and Gerhard Held were great chaps. At first, when I put them in charge of this improvised 'POW cage' in which they had a room of their own, they would jump up like jacks-in-the-box and snap to attention when I appeared. I told them not to be so formal, relax, stay seated, and they were so impressed by this friendly English informality in contrast to the sharp German discipline they had been used to that we immediately became friends. We sometimes sat together and they would tell me stories from their life in the German army. I issued them with passes so they could move freely to get rations, for which I did not have the slightest authority! At times during the war I had to use my initiative.

These two German POWs held Colin in the highest regard. When they finally left Corfu, they gave Colin two watercolours of Corfu which they had painted themselves, one of the small fort near the old town. He still has them to this day.[28] On one painting they had written on the back: 'As a memento of two German soldiers'. On the other, the inscription reads, translated from German:

> Have nothing else to give you,
> Take this from friendships hand
> As a keepsake to remember
> When we were on Corfu's strand.

> Signed Robert Neher and Gerhard Held.

Different incidents during this period remain in Colin's memory for this period, such as the time a German seaman had jumped ship:

> He took up residence with a lady in the town. When he got terribly drunk, his legs would go like rubber and it was terribly difficult to transport him out

of the way of the partisans who were unpredictable, especially with regard to Germans. One day he came to us in floods of tears because his mate, also a seaman, had gone out with a pistol. The partisans got hold of him, killed him and threw his body into the moat of the small fort. There was nothing we could do of course. Things at this time were fluid and quite chaotic as shown by another incident when we were staying at the three-star hotel. One evening a German soldier suddenly burst into the lounge, wildly looked about him, spotted the upright piano standing across a corner of the room, stepped up on the piano stool and the keyboard with a discordant clang, and leapt into the corner to hide behind the piano. He was closely followed by two partisans with guns at the ready. We told them off for invading our billet uninvited, and they reluctantly withdrew. The German thanked us profusely, and we kept him with us for a while, until the coast was clear. I cannot remember what we did about him afterwards, but the incident illustrates the electric atmosphere of those days.

At the end of October 1944, the detachment moved from the small three-star hotel to be stationed for a while in the Summer palace *Mon Repos*, the birthplace of the future Prince Philip, duke of Edinburgh. Colin found that the people of Corfu were extremely friendly and spoke exquisite English. There was even a cricket club. He found the food not brilliant, but the aged cook at *Mon Repos* called Spiro, 'managed to do wonders with beef and army biscuits. As well as the food shortage, we were short of our own rations, but presently the lobsters were ripe, as were the fruit and vegetables.' In conjunction with the Chief of Police, Colin was involved in the evacuation of the Italian civilian population and fascist administrators who were not popular with the local Greeks who were housed in a local prison for their own protection. It was the only sour note for Colin in an otherwise wonderful time on Corfu. There was much interaction with different types of groups at this time, as Colin recalls:

On Corfu at this time, there were the Royal Partisans and Communist Partisans. The Greek partisan groups were EAM (National Liberation Front), ELAS (Peoples' Liberation Army), KKE (Kapa Kapa Epsylon – Communist Party of Greece) and a company of Evzones, the Greek Royal Guards, dressed in British-style battledress, not tutus and bobbles on their shoes as peacetime palace guards. I became friendly with one Evzone guardsman called Vangi Kanelakis. Handsome and with a magnificent black beard, he spoke the most beautiful English I have ever heard. As it was beginning to get quite cold, Vangi asked me for my 'cap comforter', the kind of woollen hat which can also serve as a scarf, and gave me some Ioannina silver filigree costume jewellery in exchange which, in the fullness of time, I gave to my friend Pat Cleland back in Liverpool. These were exciting times. Vangi and I were sitting at the same table in a café when the editor of the local newspaper suddenly stood on his chair, pulled out a gun and banged holes in the ceiling. This conversation on his table had got rather heated!

On another occasion, all the dignitaries of the church came out and mixed with the partisans. But the most memorable occasion was the Feast day of St Spiridon himself, the patron saint of the island. I had the honour of meeting him during the procession. He was in a crystal glass case, standing up in his robes with mitre on, being carried by four or six monks in a procession. He was in pretty good shape and well preserved! Church treasures had been brought out for the procession alongside him. It was quite a sight. A section of our marines was invited to take part and they slow marched with bayonets fixed. It was all rather spectacular and electric in atmosphere. The mayor gave a speech from the balcony which had been draped in tapestries. The mayor turned to the commanding officer of No. 2 Brigade and offered Corfu to the British Crown. Our CO had to be very tactful in gently expressing the honour of the gesture but declining saying it depended on the British government. He got out of that tricky situation very well. It would have been insulting to have refused outright, so he was extremely diplomatic.

On another occasion Colin and a marine were invited to the wedding of the daughter of the police chief, Lieutenant Stephen Johannides, with whom he became friends. Lt Johannides and Colin had arranged the evacuation of the Italian civilians together. The wedding turned out to be quite embarrassing because amidst much dancing and drinking, the two of them were seated on two chairs like thrones. As the guests were dancing, they pinned money on the bride's dress as was the custom. 'But,' comments Colin, 'we did not have any money, so they tactfully overlooked this.' The atmosphere could become extremely tense on Corfu at this time:

On the Greek mainland, a civil war had broken out between the centre right government, and the communists who wanted to exploit the post-occupation turbulence after the demise of the right-wing administration which had collaborated with the German occupation authorities. The communists were supported by the communist Balkan regimes, Yugoslavia, Albania and Bulgaria; the British supported the government forces. The RAF ended up machine-gunning communist positions. It was a very tricky time. We were conscious that this should not spill over into Corfu, so I always made a point of mixing with the local people and never carried weapons.

The time came to leave Corfu around mid-November 1944 and Colin returned to mainland Italy. The Brigade returned to its base in Monopoli in southern Italy. In December 1944 three of Colin's colleagues from 3 Troop, Ken Bartlett, David Stewart and Alfred Shelley, arrived at the base to recruit and train a German-speaking commando unit which would be called '3 Troop Detachment'. It would be a half-troop and consist of German-speakers. Colin explains:

> The detachment would fulfil the same role as we had during the rest of the war. Now in the rank of sergeant, I was assigned to the unit to help with the training. My best friend Ken Bartlett was now a lieutenant and in charge of the detachment, with David Stewart and Alfred Shelley, also now officers. When I went to the Offiers' Mess to welcome Ken it felt like taking my life in my hands. Being New Year's Eve, all hell seemed to have broken loose. Drunken officers were roaring songs, smashing mirrors, and playing boisterous games like having to negotiate an obstacle course built from overturned furniture without touching the floor. I was directed to a room where Ken was blissfully asleep, resting from the long journey. It was a happy reunion.

From there, Ken, Colin, David and Alfred billeted themselves in the hilltop village of Minervino Murge near Bari, on the edge of the plain of Andria. They made themselves comfortable in the school on a main square:

> There was a loudspeaker system installed in the building, and I used it every morning to wake up my charges, wish them Good Morning and read out a news summary (gleaned from the radio) in BBC style. I was largely responsible for weapons training, drill, speed marches among other disciplines. At one time, perhaps brought on by shouting orders all day, I lost my voice and had to have a corporal with me to whom to whisper orders which he would then shout them out for me.

The plain of Andria became their hunting ground for training the new half-troop. By now, they knew full well how to train the new recruits and copied their own training exercises from Aberdovy and Achnacarry. That was when Colin realised just how fit he had become. He laughs as he comments: 'The new recruits had a bit of a job keeping up with us.' Years later Colin met one of them in London and the recruit said: 'Oh yes, you were our torturer.' Colin felt that was a flattering compliment in a way. Ken Bartlett planned out a very full training programme which included cross-country marches, map reading, weapons training, compass marches and field craft. The training schedules from 25 February 1945 until 24 March 1945 have survived amongst Colin's private papers and reproduced as appendices at the end of the book. One night's exercise, conducted by Alfred Shelley in a ravine, was dramatically called 'Death Valley':

> It was designed to teach our trainees to recognise the sound of different weapons in the dark. I might load a British army rifle with the distinctive sound of its bolt action, but then fire a single round from a Bren light machine gun which has a more hollow sound than the rifle shot, followed by the bang of a thunder flash and the fierce rattle of a German MG42 light machine gun.

It was in early 1945 that Colin had been granted privilege leave and chosen to stay in Rome because he wanted to see the city. It was to be another memorable period in his life because it was then that he first met a beautiful Italian girl, Livia. They embarked on a passionate love affair. During that first visit to Rome, Colin stayed in a military leave camp on the Via Appia, south of the Colosseum. He recalls the moment he first set eyes on Livia:

> I was having a cup of coffee in an open air café in the Piazza Colonna. Very untypical for Rome in January or February time a flurry of snow, almost a mini blizzard, whipped around the corner. Everyone ran for cover and I took shelter in the colonnade around the Piazza, when my eye was caught by the spectacular beauty of a young woman in elegant fur coat and hat, with an older lady. I gathered all my courage and went up to her. We had been looking at each other. I apologised for accosting her, but asked whether she could give me some advice because the leave camp was fine but I would prefer to be out of the military atmosphere for my two weeks' leave. I asked whether she knew of anyone who could let a room. She eyed me up and down and said that her mother sometimes let out a room in their flat across the river. She suggested I follow her home and speak with her mother. As we were crossing the Ponte Cavour, to my surprise we were already arm-in-arm. For a well bred lady to be seen so close with a foreign soldier might not have been desirable.
>
> We finally arrived at her elegant apartment in the Via Muzio Clementi. Her mother was out, so we went one floor up to the flat of her companion, who turned out to be a chaperone and friend. Before long, Livia was sitting on my knee and we were getting extremely friendly. After her mother came home, she was happy to let a room to me. I stayed there for the rest of my leave. Livia and I became exceedingly close. Livia was a startling, Roman beauty with lovely black hair and eyes. I fell heavily in love with her. She was very passionate and needless to say I didn't see much more of Rome.

In spite of being preoccupied and in love, Colin managed to visit the Vatican and the Sistine Chapel during his period of leave. He was also amongst one of 300 people in a private audience inside the Vatican with His Holiness Pope Pius XII (formerly Cardinal Pacelli). The Pope gave a short speech in English, then French and a longer speech in Italian. Those present were then blessed before they left. The rest of the time Colin spent with Livia.

After two weeks he had to return to his unit. Correspondence with Livia was impossible because of the war. It was a long time before he could see her again. Through friends who went on leave to Rome, Colin sent Livia gifts, usually a tin of something not easy to get in wartime. Some time later he was on leave again. He headed straight for Rome:

As our truck got near to Rome, so my heart beat faster and faster. I was nearly choking with excitement. My second visit took place after we had moved North, in April, after conclusion of our training programme. We travelled by train in a goods wagon, and stopped overnight in a goods yard outside Rome. I was of course not allowed to leave, although so close to Livia that I almost fancied I could smell her perfume. Torture! Not made easier by Ken laughing at this lovelorn swain clinging to the chain link fence round the goods yard, gazing at the glow of the metropolis in the night sky. As soon as I could, I went straight to Livia's flat, knocked on the door. Livia opened it and we fell into each other's arms. We spent another happy, passionate leave together.

During this time I maintained contact with the driver of the truck who had dropped me off in Rome and taken my other comrades to the leave camp. I was in charge of this group and arranged pick-up again with the driver. We agreed that there was a technical fault with the truck so our return journey was delayed by a couple of days and I could spend more time with Livia. With Livia, it was an intense love affair. When I left, she gave me a picture of the Virgin and Child. On the back she had written: '*Perchè la Madonna ti proteggia da ogni pericolo!*' (May the Madonna protect you from all peril). I wore it over my heart!

On 2 April 1945, the troop detachment received its marching orders. Amongst Colin's papers are 3 Troop Moving Orders for this period, which read:

Dress: Battledress, Berets, Gaiters, Personal Weapons, Webbing-Equipment

Small Pack (to be worn on left side) containing: Gascape folded and overlapping, Mess tin, knife, fork, spoon, housewife, spare pair socks, laces, washing & shaving kit, rations.

Large pack, containing: groundsheet, folded and overlapping, pullover, greatcoat, spare belt, 1 blanket.

Steel helmets will be carried under the straps of large pack
Water bottles will be carried on the right side
Respirators will be packed in kit-bag.

They moved to the front in the north of Italy, now preparing for the crossing of the Po delta. They were billeted not far from Ravenna, south of Valli di Commacchio. The last actions in that area were the Argenta Gap. This was the gap between flooded areas where the dykes had been destroyed or opened by the Germans to flood the area as a last defensible barrier from advancing troops:

That cost casualties to break through the Argenta Gap. Valli di Commacchio is a muddy lagoon on the east coast of Italy. In order to take the land which divides the lagoon from the Adriatic, they used Buffalos, amphibious armoured personnel carriers. They intended to carry the troops across the lagoon to the spit of land which was being tenaciously defended. It was not a straightforward crossing, as the water was so shallow that the vehicles tended to build up a wall of mud in front of them, but eventually they got through. Although they were not tanks, they looked impressive and made a lot of noise. When they appeared in the rear of the enemy position, resistance collapsed, the Germans surrendered. I was not actually part of this push. I was back in the village where we had temporarily been billeted but once the Germans had surrendered, we took about 1,200 POWs. But it turned out that they were not Germans as such. They had a shield on their sleeve marked 'Brigade Georgien'. They were Georgians who had been Soviet POWs who had been taken by the Germans. They didn't like the Russians, so it had been relatively easy to recruit the Georgians into the German army. Now we found ourselves faced with 1,200 POWs in German uniform, none of whom could speak German except a lieutenant who spoke patchy and broken German. We sent him off in a jeep to the rear somewhere to be interrogated.

Colin soon became extremely busy dealing with the surrendering German army in the north of Italy. The scene was one of masses of German forces in disarray, their military vehicles out of diesel being towed by the only ones that had fuel left in their tanks:

We fenced off fields on the Ravenna plain in this very flat part of Italy. The surrendering German POWs sat in row after row as far as the eye could see. I started by taking down names, took their money and gave them a receipt for it. They had Italian occupation money which was not worth anything anymore. I soon stopped making a list because it was impossible to cope with the sheer numbers. There was no where for them to escape anyway. I was amongst them all day and night; the first three days with virtually no sleep. We tried to lay on some rations for them; brought in water tankers so at least they could fill their water bottles. It was towards morning of one day that I got back to the bungalow where I was billeted. I stripped off, dashed straight across the beach and into the water. It was so refreshing. As I came back and opened the door, I recoiled because it was full of a pungent smell of Germans. I had been amongst the German soldiers so long that my clothes had begun to smell like them. It was a distinctive, rather acrid aroma made up of the smell of leather equipment, uniform material, sweat, *Jagdwurst* and other food from their diet. It was an unmistakable smell. In fact during the war, this distinctive smell saved lives because as soon as you got a whiff of it, you knew to take cover because there were Germans in the area.

One of the men in Colin's troop, who had been in a concentration camp before the war, recognised a guard from that camp amongst the surrendering troops. 'He went ballistic,' says Colin. They checked him and found that he had the standard SS tattoos, so handed him to the military authorities for interrogation. He was on the run and had tried to hide amongst the mass of Waffen SS. In those first few days, long hours in the heat meant that Colin soon became extremely tired and had no time to shave. It was whilst in this slightly dishevelled state that a significant incident occurred:

Whilst I was rushing about, dealing with the POWs, trying to cope with the situation with my comrades, there appeared a small column of *Kübelwagen*, the open-top field command cars. It pulled into our field and stopped. In the front car there sat a German general, stony faced, looking over the heads of everybody. He didn't move a muscle. I was too busy to attend to him. He began to go a bright red colour, rising from his collar. It was the same colour as his red collar with the golden wheat sheaves symbol on. It rose into his cheeks and suddenly he shouted, in that peculiar crowing tone sometimes adopted by high-ranking officers: '*Ja, was ist denn hier los? Ist denn hier kein Lagerkommandant? Ich bin ein GenerAAAL!*' [What's the matter here? Is there no camp commandant? I'm a General!] And on the word 'General' he almost hit the top C.

Colin approached him in denision smock (a parachute smock without badges of rank) and Green Beret, plus a day's stubble and said to him in a similar tone of command in which he may not have been addressed since he was a cadet at Spandau: '*Abwarten! Ihre Leute kommen zuerst dran!*' (Wait for it! Your men come first.) It produced a reaction:

I have never seen a jaw drop quite so far so quickly as that general that day. He was horrified and indignant. I pointed out the camp commandant's tent a couple of fields away and asked them to report to him. Upon which one of them turned round to the front row of soldiers sitting in the grassy field and said: '*Feldwebel! Drei Mann zum Gepäcktragen!*' [Sergeant, three men to carry luggage]. I quickly replied, '*Feldwebel, bleiben Sie sitzen.*' [Sergeant, stay seated]. I then turned to the officers and said, 'Gentlemen, you will take such luggage as you can carry yourselves.' They looked deflated, took off their smart uniform jackets, and underneath they were wearing khaki shirts and braces. They were no longer quite as impressive. They had to carry their own luggage. As I watched them, I felt slightly ashamed at being so rude to them, but on the other hand I really felt it was quite inappropriate under the circumstances for a German general to start ordering me about. I was now in charge.

The following day Colin was scheduled to accompany a cavalcade of cars to take the high-ranking Nazi officers to Bologna. 'To my great shame, I overslept,' he says. Someone came and woke him up just in time. He managed to rush out and merge just as they were leaving. He and another soldier sat on two dicky-seats facing each other, Tommy guns at the ready, behind the German officers on the back seats of the staff car, with British officers in the other seats. He and his comrade were the armed guard escort to take them to the formal surrender point for the Germans of high rank:

Once in Bologna, I took the opportunity to go into a barbershop to be tidied up. Afterwards, while the others were awaiting for the general officers to emerge from the capitulation conference, I started to chat to a very smart German soldier with medals and prestigious badges. I was called back by one of our officers and informed that I was not to fraternise with the enemy!

That was the end of the war for Colin. After this, he stayed in Ravenna for a short time longer. He was able to relax some evenings with the local people, most of whom had 'adopted' the British soldiers as their family. Colin recalls one charming incident:

In Ravenna, I was sitting outside one day with 'my family' when we were joined by a neighbour. We all chatted and enjoyed the lovely warm evening until late. Suddenly the mother laughed and turned to me and said: 'do you know what she [the neighbour] has just me? She asked whether you came from Rome.' And was I proud! I have Livia to thank for learning a good Italian pronunciation. Her family came from Tuscany, where they speak a good grammatical Italian but in a rather flat accent, but she grew up in Rome where their speech is beautifully musical. As the Italians say: the best Italian is '*Lingua Toscana in bocca Romana!*' [The language of Tuscany in the mouth of Rome.]

The war had entered its final stages. German forces were disintegrating, apart from last-ditch attempts by diehard Nazis to defend Germany. On 30 April 1945 Adolf Hitler was dead, having committed suicide in his bunker with new wife Eva Braun. Allied forces had liberated the concentration camps, revealing to the world the full extent of the horror of the mass extermination of 6 million Jews and 5 million others. Across Western Europe, Allied forces had liberated France, Belgium and Holland. Finally they had invaded Germany, captured Hamburg and entered Berlin. Germany was forced to sign unconditional surrender. 8 May 1945 was celebrated as VE Day – Victory in Europe. At this time Colin was still on the east coast of Italy, billeted in a small bungalow at Bellaria, right on the beach, while trying to sort out the flood of surrendering German soldiers:

It was during this time that I borrowed a motorcycle because I had to visit colleagues located further north who were looking after a surrendered Waffen SS unit. The transport NCO satisfied himself that I could manage the machine, though I had never ridden a motorbike before, and lent me the appropriate crash helmet to go with it. My bicycling experience helped, and I enjoyed the ride along the straight, empty road on a beautiful, sunny afternoon. I cannot remember the purpose of the visit, but I came across a group of worried-looking young German women who were the companions of the SS men. I overheard one of them saying to another: 'Oh, look – they are going to hang us!' pointing at some British soldiers erecting tall poles. I reassured them that we were not SS, and that we did not hang people, but that the poles were for a chain link fence. Maybe I should have let them stew for a bit longer; but perhaps it may have helped them to understand the difference between the mentality of SS Nazis and normal, civilised people?

When I went to start the motorbike for my return trip, one soldier bet me that I would have great difficulty – the army motorbikes were notoriously awkward to start when the engine was warm. Luckily for me it sprang to life with my first kick!

For Colin, suddenly the war came to an end:

It was rather a shock. It was expected that everyone would celebrate and go wild. What actually happened was quite the opposite. We were all very subdued and rather depressed. It was as though the firm you had worked for, for the last six years had gone bankrupt. I went for a lonely walk through the night time streets of Ravenna and then back to the Sergeant's Mess. We had listened to Churchill on the wireless. It was all over.

In stirring words, Prime Minister Winston Churchill's broadcast praised the Allied forces and told the people:

This is your victory! It is the victory of the cause of freedom in every land. In all our long history we have never seen a greater day than this. Everyone, man or woman, has done their best. Neither the long years, nor the dangers, nor the fierce attacks of the enemy, have in any way weakened the independent resolve of the British nation.

From Ravenna, Colin then transferred with his unit by goods train to Naples in order to embark for their return to England. The weather was warm:

We had organised some furniture to take on the train with us, i.e. comfortable chairs. We kept the large sliding doors of the train wide open so we could enjoy the journey in the comfortable chairs. We had a bucket of sand with petrol in it to brew up tea as we travelled. At one time when the flame started to die down, one of our men had the bright idea of topping up the bucket straight from the petrol can, which promptly caught fire. I had my back to it in my comfortable chair, but another member of our group picked up the flaming petrol can and, in one smooth movement, flung it past me out of the open door. It exploded on the side of the cutting through which we were travelling at the time. The name of our saviour was Stephens, a Swiss national who had previously served in the French Foreign Legion and was recruited for the troop in Italy. A first-class soldier; I always felt he should have been our sergeant, not I. Instead of the sand bucket, we then made our tea by putting the ingredients into a large empty army biscuit tin and, during our frequent stops, taking it up to the engine where the driver would indicate a tube where to hold the tin while he opened a valve, sending a steaming jet of boiling water into our tin. Instant tea!

In Naples they were taken to a tented embarkation camp and informed they were sailing back to England on an American ship. Colin was still with his friends Ken Bartlett, Shelley and Stewart. They learnt that the ship was dry: i.e. no alcohol on board. It was a disappointment:

We had just drawn our rations and had bottles of whisky. We had thought we would have an agreeable trip home. Whilst in Italy, I had acquired an old-fashioned officers' camp bed. It was rather heavy with scissor frame. The night before we embarked, I went to bed in my camp bed and drank the whole bottle of whisky! One of our group came in, waving his bottle, heavily sat down on my bed which dissolved into a heap. It was a memorable night!

It was the first time in six years that Colin had been on a ship that was not in convoy. It landed at Southampton. As they passed the Isle of Wight all the troops on board crowded the port side of the deck for their first view of English soil. For some of them who had been in North Africa before Italy, it had been years since they had seen the English coast:

And the ship tilted over to the left. And as we rounded the isle and entered the Solent close to the Hampshire shore, everyone rushed over to the right and the ship heeled over to starboard. As they spotted policeman cycling along the shoreline path, a great cheer went up. He waved his helmet in greeting, shouted 'What lot are you?' and with one voice the whole ship roared back 'D-Day Dodgers!' [A reference to a tactless remark made in Parliament by Lady Nancy Astor]. But of course we had all had a few landings under our belt in Italy and Sicily.

Colin then travelled to Liverpool while on disembarkation leave, heading straight to see his adopted family, the Clelands. Among his gifts to Pat was a 'five-pointed star' partisan cap-badge of one of Tito's Partisans. 'She really appreciated this,' he comments, 'because of her communist ideals at that time.' From Liverpool, Colin then travelled to Seaford in Sussex. There was little to do there, but they continued training to keep occupied:

Since we had to do something to pass the time and to keep up in case we should be sent to the Far East, we tended to do compass marches like the ones we did in training. After progressing on the various bearings for the prescribed distances, we tended to arrive at a lunchtime destination to find that on the map it would be marked 'Inn'. But for tea we tended to aim at Alfriston.

As soon as the Japanese surrendered, the commandos were dissolved. Major General Laycock, Chief of Combined Operations, paid tribute to the international troop of No.10 Inter-Allied Commando and wrote:

To those of the famous but mysterious International Troop, our special gratitude is due, for they fought with equal daring by the side of their British comrades.[29]

Colin travelled to London on leave and celebrated VJ Day in the capital:

> Spending VJ day in London was very exciting. I was in the crowd in front of
> Buckingham Palace, climbed up the Victoria Memorial but was politely asked
> to get down by a policeman. The King and Queen came out on the balcony, as
> did Churchill. It was a euphoric moment.

Colin learned the fate of members of 3 Troop. Casualty rates were high; so too
fatalities, mainly in Normandy during and after the landings. Lieutenant Peter
Wells (Werner Auerhahn) was killed in action in Italy on 19 January 1944.
Max Laddy (Max Lewinsky) and Webster (Weinberger) were killed on D-Day
on Sword Beach before they made it ashore. George MacFranklyn (Max
Frank), who had survived being wounded in action in Italy and posted with 4
Commando for the Normandy invasion, was killed by a mortar on the beach
on D-Day. Eugene Fuller (Eugen von Kagerer-Stein) was wounded on D-Day
and died on 13 June. Ernest Lawrence (Ernst Lenel) was reported missing in
action. His body was never recovered and he is commemorated on the Bayeux
Memorial in Normandy. Richard Arlen (R. Abramovicz) was killed in action at
Franceville-Plage on 7 June 1944; Kenneth Graham (Kurt Gumpertz) on 12–13
June; Frederick Fletcher (F. Fleischer) at Le Plein on 11 June 1944; Peter Moody
(Kurt Meyer) died in Normandy on 13 June; Ernest Norton (Ernst Nathan), who
was attached to 4 Commando, was also killed on 13 June; and Harry Andrews
(Hans Arnstein) in August 1944 killed by an S-mine while leading a patrol. Capt.
Robert Hamilton (Salo Reich) was killed at Walcheren on 1 November 1944 and
Herbert Seymour (H. Sachs) crossing the Rhine on 23 March 1945. Eric Howard
(Erich Nathan) was wounded in action on D-Day, commissioned in the field for
bravery but was killed at Osnabruck on 3 April 1945. Keith Griffith (Kurt Glaser)
was killed in Germany on 11 April 1945 crossing the Aller River. Those wounded
in action included Troop Sgt Major Oscar O'Neill (Hentschel), Maurice Latimer
(Levy), Tommy Swinton (Schwytzer) and Freddie Gray (Manfred Gans). Sgt
Brian Groves (Goldschmidt) was involved in Operation *Partridge*, a raid behind
enemy lines in Italy, over the River Garigliano during the Allied advance. He
was wounded so badly that a foot had to be amputated. Steve Ross (Stephan
Rosskamm) was wounded twice in Italy. Ian Harris (Hans Hajos) was wounded
three times in Normandy, serving with 46 Royal Marine Commando.

A number of 3 Troop veterans were honoured for bravery. The skipper, Brian
Hilton-Jones, and George Lane (Georg Lanyi), a Hungarian, were both given
the Military Cross. Ian Harris was awarded the Military Medal; Robert Barnes
(Gotthard Baumwollspinner) the Distinguished Conduct Medal; and Jack Davies
(Hansen) was Mentioned in Dispatches.

Having been engaged in some of the bloodiest and most difficult actions of the war, surviving members of 3 Troop were sent back to Germany to begin the denazification process, working for British Army of the Rhine (BAOR), Control Commission or Field Security (the section responsible for hunting Nazi war criminals). All had a vital role to play in rebuilding the new democratic Germany. Their knowledge of, and fluency in, the German language was crucial to the Allied occupying forces. They spent at least a year, sometimes longer, fulfilling their final duties in British Army uniform. Colin was posted to Germany with British Control Commission. He was about to set foot on German soil for the first time in six years.

CHAPTER 9

Return to Frankfurt

s soon as Colin knew he was being sent back to Germany, he requested to be posted to Frankfurt to find his mother. He had high hopes that she had survived the war and come through the Allied bombing of Frankfurt.

Prior to leaving for Germany, Colin was required to report to the London headquarters of the Control Commission to receive his latest vaccinations. He and his mates were very blasé about the injections because in six years in the army, they had been given so many jabs. He comments: 'That was a bit dangerous because if we were not tensed up beforehand, and then did not have the defence against the physical shock when the needle goes in. Every one of our lot nearly fainted. Everyone else in the queue was fine, except us – the tough commandos!' For a short time, Colin and other ex-refugee German-speakers had to report to a house south of London's Hyde Park where a retired cavalry general was supposed to train them for their posting to Germany. The general's first reaction was how ridiculous it was that he was to teach them German. Instead, he recounted stories of his time in the army. Colin's request to be stationed in Frankfurt was granted. He was sent to work with Field Intelligence Agency Technical (FIAT) in the British enclave at Höchst near Frankfurt. It was here that his fluency in German was to be used in an aspect of the denazification process:

We were billeted in the small village of Sindlingen. All kinds of personnel were attached to FIAT for various duties under the charge of Colonel Davson. Most of them, both men and women, had been in the forces. I was assigned to

Colonel Davson as his personal assistant. It was an extremely interesting time because we translated all kinds of documentation, mostly to do with industry, science, medical progress, and some military matters. Half of my time approx was spent translating these documents, the other half was spent travelling all over Germany, having contact with German scientists or industrialists. I spent time working with interesting professionals from Britain who were at the peak of their careers and had come to Germany to exchange notes with their counterparts: doctors, visiting German generals in the Medical Corps, as well as liaising with surgeons and industrial scientists. I acted as translator for them. We made contact with their German counterparts, with whom they had had no communication during the six years of war. I prided myself to get to the stage where I got ignored, so that people began talking to each other, not realising that there was an interpreter (me) in between. I visited underground factories in Bavaria, met high-grade medical people in the company of a medical brigadier that I was interpreter for. It was a very rewarding time.

There was one single most important task for Colin – to search for his mother. At the earliest opportunity he returned to the address where she was last known to be living.

For his mother, it was not quite such a shock because Colin's closest friend Ken Bartlett had already passed through Frankfurt and made it his business to call on her. Ken visited her on 14 September 1945 and relayed to her the good news that her son was a soldier in the British Army and had come through the war alive. Afterwards Ken travelled to Cologne where he was stationed with radio in the British sector. What Colin did not know as he travelled to Frankfurt in search of his mother was that she had already written to him. She had given a standard Red Cross letter consisting of twenty-five words via an American solider who had passed through Frankfurt. It was hoped that the letter would make it to Colin's half-sister Suzanne in New York and eventually to Colin himself. Unfortunately, the Red Cross never forwarded the letter to Colin. It read:

> Dearest Claus. Alive in half-ruined flat. Only sign of life: Bara. Mori totally burned out. Six year's postal work at an end. Great longing to hear from you. Your Mother.

In late August, early September 1945, the American soldier also carried a further lengthy letter from Mrs Ascher to her son and Suzanne. Neither did this letter reach Colin at that time, but he does have it in his possession today. In that letter his mother describes how she survived the war in Germany. It provides a revealing insight into life in wartime Germany and the conditions that she suffered.

All neighbouring houses had been destroyed or burnt. Her roof and walls suffered damage, and repair was all but impossible in spite of the best efforts of a friendly handyman, as materials were impossible to obtain. There was much strategic deployment of buckets, bowls and an umbrella in wet weather. But even so she continued to 'look on the bright side' and described her life in a positive way. She had come to like her lofty eyrie with its views and the song of the blackbirds:

Dear Suzanne, dear Claus,

At last there is an opportunity for me to send an indication that I am alive to New York, and you, dear Suzanne, will no doubt be able to forward them on to Claus of whom I have had no news for years and am anxiously waiting to hear whether both of you and also your mother are alive, whether you are doing well and how Claus may have coped with his life and circumstances. I asked an American soldier about the possibility of forwarding a letter to NY, and it turned out that he himself will be travelling to NY before the end of this month (September), so I may hope that this letter will reach you.

Well, so I have escaped alive through all the horrors, running for my life down bomb shelter or cellar and total destruction of nearly all neighbouring houses by fire. How often were we lying on the floor while the house shook, hellish noise roaring outside, the stovepipe shot out of the wall, clinging quite uselessly with both hands to the table leg, and so on. If the lights went out immediately we would know that this time it is Frankfurt's turn. Then there would be knocking to open the escape hatch, and the neighbours would flee from the ruins of their house to us.

I worked for a long time at the postal distribution centre at the Frankfurt East railway station in the small packets distribution section. There sometimes we had to crowd into a passage full of water pipes if the ground attack aircraft did not leave us enough time to run along the platform to the bunker (lately picking our way around wreckage).

You wrote at one time that I had forgotten to write what I was working at: I did not dare to, as one time I had already been summarily dismissed as the widow of a Jewish man who 'had not even divorced him'. Some higher official did re-employ me that time, but with disciplinary transfer to the Frankfurt East station to heavy labour. However, there I was able to join training courses and to obtain a somewhat better position. But it was very unpleasant that we had fewer and fewer men and we therefore had to act as porters, carrying heavy loads every day. Some of us nearly broke down physically, especially as in Germany so many women suffer from heart or gallbladder complaints. But I doggedly stuck it out without, thank God, any particular physical complaints, until now we have all been sacked due to lack of work. At present I am giving some English lessons as I am reasonably competent in English, but now I must try to get a permanent job again.

Shortly before the catastrophe RM 3000 was sent to me, which belongs to me. But they never arrived and probably I shall have to accept the loss, since the only authority to which you could apply for compensation is the German Reich, which would be pretty futile. As there no longer was any other way, the bank sent it in cash in a registered letter, and either the Nazis pocketed it, or it was part of what was destroyed when the Nazis burnt everything they found in the post offices. I had always received RM 60 from my brother, but for a long time now all communication within Germany has broken down. However, I did receive a post card a few days ago by a circuitous route, a sign of life from my sister, Aunt Bara. She survived, but has moved to a crowded Pension, as most of Bremen has been destroyed. My brother's house has been burnt to the ground. He and his wife are now at Dohnsen, a family estate where my sister-in-law has a right of residence.

So far as my flat is concerned, we residents are delighted every day that the house still exists, in the middle of nothing but ruins. Only, the roof has had a hundred thousand holes for as long as one can remember, which cannot be mended owing to shortage of materials. The bedroom is totally uninhabitable. I sleep one floor below, but there, too, the rain splashes through in various places. In the sitting room/kitchen I cook by electricity since the current has been restored. There I sit at my table and feel at home, while round about me the raindrops are rattling into the containers placed round-about, and sometimes a lump of clay may land on my arm or neck. I am proud of the fact that a short time ago the husband of a friend at work has fixed a window where for such a long time there had been an open hole. Unfortunately he was unable to stop the cascade which pours out of the middle of the wall, close to it.

The food situation is dire. I don't want to complain, as here in Germany we clearly must limit our expectations. But it is wretched when the weekly 5 lbs potato ration is 3 or 4 weeks in arrears and could then be cancelled, while at the same time there is no flour, never enough bread, no sugar , hardly any butter, no other kind of fat, hardly any meat. Of course, I shan't even mention anything like coffee, tea, eggs.

So now you know that so far I am among the survivors, although you might be surprised by my appearance. I weigh about 105 lbs, compared with a normal weight of 165 lbs, and in the past even 185 lbs. With this self-portrait I shall bring this letter to an end.

Heartfelt greetings and kisses to you, dear Suzanne, and to you, my Big [Claus's nickname] who I hope is well, from your M-P [initials of nickname]

P.S: I'm afraid I have to inform you, dear Claus, that your cello, mattress and remaining furniture etc. were burnt in Mrs. Wüst's completely destroyed house. She herself moved out of town, but is now again in Frankfurt during the week, in the position of detective inspector which was her rank before 1933. It was she who had arranged for the money to be sent, at my request.

The day came when Colin walked along once familiar streets of Frankfurt, a city that had been devastated by Allied bombing. He stood outside the address in Hermann Strasse where his mother was known to be living. He entered the building:

I started up the stairs and heard my mother coming down from the top floor. I knew it was her because she had a distinctive footstep which I recognised immediately. In order to prevent a sudden shock for her on stairs, as she turned the corner, I rushed up and embraced her. And she said '*Nanu!*' (Good Lord! What's all this?) She saw a British soldier with a green beret on and presumed it was my friend Ken Bartlett, whom she had seen weeks before in the same uniform. Then I said, 'No, I have the honour of being your son, madam.' We had a great laugh. It was a relief to be reunited. We went up to her room in the attic and caught up on as much as we could. It was a wonderful reunion – more joyous than emotional shedding of tears.

Thereafter Colin visited his mother whenever he could, bringing her gifts from the sergeants' mess, coffee and such things. Frankfurt was in the American occupation zone, but FIAT, based outside of Höchst in the original IG Farben headquarters and the village of Sindlingen, was in effect a British enclave. When he was in the American sector, the rations were much better than the British rations: 'Whenever I visited my Mess in Sindlingen, between Höchst and Mainz, you could hear people groan: "oh, no, not chicken again".' Although Colin was in the American sector, he only worked with British personnel. It was a mixed bunch at Sindlingen:

We had civilians (the Green Lizards) working with us, so called because of the green insignia on the epaulettes of their battledress, marking them out as civilian members of the Control Commission. There were also people from all services looking for the perpetrators of the Stalag Luft III massacre, the execution of recaptured escapees from the RAF officers' POW camp of that name. When I wasn't travelling, I was able to go into Frankfurt and be with my mother, also pick up with good friends from my childhood, especially violinist Gustav Lenzewski and his wife Ina who were a great help and support to my mother during the war. I was also able to see old friends from the BK (Protestant Youth

Group), including Kurt-Helmut Schlichtegroll (who had marched all down the Norwegian coast, including every fjord and inlet, when the German army withdrew). He in particular arranged reunions with survivors. I paid a visit to Albert Hamel to thank him for the great debt I owed him and for teaching me about the epic poem *Die Füsse im Feuer*.

From FIAT, Colin was sent twice on a visit to Berlin for a week or two at a time. He recalls that period:

> I travelled to Berlin in a very luxurious train with sleepers and diners; satin finished stainless steel everywhere. While the train was stopped at Helmstedt, the border crossing between the western and soviet zones, we were being served with a sumptuous American breakfast of eggs and bacon, waffles dripping with syrup. All the while we were being watched through the plate-glass windows of our dining car by a crowd of hungry Germans packing the platform in the hope of the occasional American cigar butt. In Berlin, I was driven in a Volkswagen to my billets and accommodated in a flat with balconies. I was stationed in a flat in affluent West Berlin, which was in the British Zone. Life was normal for the people there. The rest of Berlin had been pretty much devastated and razed to the ground by the Allied bombing in the war, but where I was stationed, it was largely untouched. But as an Allied soldier I had access to East Berlin which was in the Soviet Zone. I went there to visit a sister of my father's who was married to an 'Aryan' called Müller. They lived in an eastern part of Berlin, called Karlshorst, close to the Soviet headquarters. Their sons, Hans-Rudolf and Peter, had served in auxiliary army units (which 'mixed-race' half-Jewish sons of Aryan fathers could do). But we had not been in touch because it was felt they had cosied-up to the Nazis. I would not hold it against them now, but at the time it angered my father.

Colin's task in Berlin was to translate documentation from the records of Berlin-based Ministry of Weapons and Equipment which had been under Albert Speer. Speer was later amongst the Nazi war criminals on trial at Nuremberg. For his work, Colin was allocated two bilingual secretaries to get through the volume of documents for the Allies:

> I rattled off chunks of documentation, translating for the secretaries to type up. We got through a lot of dictation work in the morning; then in the afternoon I dictated to the other secretary, whilst the first one transcribed the morning's work. It proved to be fascinating work because of the contents of the documents, much dealing with the development of new German

weaponry. One was a sub-machine gun which could fire round the corner with a little mirror [periscope] and a curved barrel with increased bore going around so the bullet could get around a corner at close range. This would be very useful in street fighting to stay undercover whilst shooting around a corner. The centrifugal casting techniques were used for artillery gun barrels. Different grades of steel would even-out different expansion co-efficients and absorb heat, and the innermost layer would be a high-grade chrome steel for wear resistance. These were just examples of many interesting and resourceful ingenuities. But the most interesting aspect was the departmental in-fighting where, for instance, the production facilities of the ammunition to suit the StG 44, the sub-machine gun/assault rifle which had the curved-barrel version, were diverted by someone outranking those who were demanding increased production. The generals were screaming for more assault rifles to provide the increased volume of fire desperately needed on the Eastern Front. Some of the documents I translated revealed this in-fighting and difference of opinion between different sections of the German military.

Back in Frankfurt after his visits to Berlin, Colin was conscious of some unfinished business. He still did not know who had betrayed his father to the Gestapo. Who had betrayed him? 'I just had to find out who denounced my father,' he comments.

Colin decided to call upon Frau Else Wüst, the woman who had been a police inspector before the Nazi period, had been re-instated after the war, and who had had a mixed relationship with his mother. Frau Wüst had been helpful in so many ways immediately after Curt Ascher's death in Dachau. Now she enabled Colin to visit the police headquarters in Frankfurt and go through the files. He came across his father's file and leafed through the papers. There in black and white was the name of the man who had betrayed his father, and effectively sentenced him to death. Colin stood at the crossroads of a moral decision:

It was a certain lock keeper called Herr Henkel who lived at Niederrad along the river Main, to the west of Sachsenhausen where I had originally worked at the Asbestos Works before my emigration. What should I do with this information? The knowledge produced a rather difficult psychological situation for me. I had a lot of discretion and authority at that time as a British staff sergeant and could pretty well do what I wanted. I could roll up outside his house in a staff car in uniform or I could go about on a bicycle in civilian clothes. I could also walk about with weapons. I could have done something about it. The temptation was undoubtedly there to pay Herr Henkel a visit, invite him for a walk in the forest south of Frankfurt, from which only I would have come back. But I never took advantage of my situation. It was not my place to take his life. Why? Because my religious upbringing reminded me that 'Revenge is mine' says the Lord, 'I will repay'.[30] I hated the Nazis, but I could not exact revenge on Herr Henkel for the death of my father. It was not my place to take another life in revenge.

Colin's Protestant upbringing, coupled with his parents' high moral standards, had a decisive effect on his decision not to take Herr Henkel's life. A story told to him by Herr Hamel whilst he was in the Protestant Youth Group BK in the 1930s now assumed particular relevance. It was the epic poem *Die Füsse im Feuer*.

The poem describes a fictional episode during the persecution of the Huguenots in sixteenth-century France. A king's messenger rides through a wild night in south-western France when he comes to a small chateau where he demands food and shelter in the king's name. He is courteously received by the owner – a dignified, elderly, widowed aristocrat who lives there in straitened circumstances, and is treated as an honoured guest with generous hospitality. After his host has shown him to a guest chamber after dinner, the messenger can't get rid of an uneasy feeling that this place is somehow familiar – and then suddenly with blinding clarity he remembers that he was here during the religious wars with a party to arrest the Huguenot marquis, who had fled or was in hiding. They interrogated his wife with increasing severity, and then resorted to torture to force the lady to reveal the whereabouts of the husband, but she refused to speak. Finally, they dragged her to the fireplace and held her feet in the flames; she still refused, and then died from the torture.

The messenger was sure her widower, whom he had now met for the first time, knew who he was and would exact revenge during the night. He barricaded the door with heavy furniture, lay on the bed fully clothed and with his bare sword to hand, and prepared to defend his life. But he was overcome by exhaustion after his strenuous ride, and fell asleep in spite of himself. He awoke with an icy shock, to find his host had entered by a tapestry door his guest had not noticed and was standing by his bed, carrying a breakfast tray for his guest – and to see that his grey hair had turned snow white overnight. And then he collected himself, smiled cynically and said 'Your lordship is wise not to think of revenge for an act carried out in the service of the king, and interfere with an officer of his majesty'. The Marquis replied: 'Mine is the vengeance, says the lord! I will repay.'

Colin comments with some emotion in his voice:

> That story remained with me all my life. It was the remembrance of the moral to that poem that influenced my decision not to exact revenge on Herr Henkel in Frankfurt at the end of the war. Through the Protestant Youth Group I had been inculcated with a very high moral standard.

Whilst stationed near Frankfurt, Colin took the opportunity to visit his father's grave. As he stood there in British army uniform to reflect, it was a poignant moment. His father would have been so very proud of him.

How had it felt to be back in Frankfurt? His emotional reaction to his return shows how in the intervening years a 'brotherhood' had emerged from his training and combat in the commandos:

> I felt perfectly at home on visits to my mother, but in Frankfurt itself I felt like a stranger. I was aware how much I had changed and how times had changed me. I no longer felt at home in a place in which I had been rather at home beforehand. As a schoolboy walking to school every day in the 1930s, I was familiar with the place and the atmosphere, it was my home town. Even though conditions were so hostile under the Nazis, I still felt at home amongst my circle of friends. But as a soldier in British army uniform, to walk these particular streets of Frankfurt with the ghost of a German schoolboy walking ahead, with whom I had absolutely nothing in common anymore, was an almost schizophrenic psychological stress. To feel that I had to get back to my own people at the mess where I could relax again, showed me how I had changed. I hadn't really expected to survive the war in the commandos, but there was a job that had to be done. I wanted to repay the debt to Britain for saving my life.

By the summer of 1946, Colin was approaching the time for his demobilisation. An outstanding reference dated 3 July 1946 was provided by Brian Hilton-Jones, ex-Major and Second-in-Command of No. 10 Commando, in which he wrote of Colin with the highest respect and regard:

> Sergeant C. E. Anson was one of a number of volunteers personally chosen by me from amongst a large body of applicants in August 1942 for special service of a particularly hazardous nature. From that time until the disbandment of the unit at the end of 1945 he served, directly and indirectly, under my command and I therefore had ample opportunity of judging him and his work. He showed himself throughout to be an extremely capable and effective soldier and NCO, and served with considerable distinction in the field. Doing his work well he always did it with a readiness and enthusiasm which, coupled with his capable reliability, made him one of the most valuable members of a unit whose average standard happened to be exceptionally high; and apart from his value to his officers he was also held in high regard by his comrades.

On 1 August that year, the head of section at FIAT wrote a glowing report of Colin's service with him:

Lt. Col. H.J.H Davson (ret), D.S.O.
Officer i/c Pool of Interpreters
Field Information Agency, Technical (Main)
HQ 69 CCG, BAOR

During my long service I have always tried to avoid superlatives in reports. I find it very hard to do so in the case of S/Sgt C.E.Anson. My department calls for a very high standard of work. It deals with every technical subject imaginable, also economics, chemistry, medicine, physics, industrial subjects etc. All my interpreters have given me satisfaction, but S/Sgt Anson stands head and shoulders above them all. His work has always been of the highest standard, and the branches for whom he has worked have the very highest opinion of him. I myself cannot praise him too highly. In the midst of the hardest work he has never shown any impatience when asked for help by weaker interpreters, but has given that help willingly. For some weeks now he has been acting as my Personal Assistant and has performed the duties with the tact and ability which I expected of him.

I have the very highest opinion of his personal character, quiet, well behaved and efficient in addition to other qualities mentioned above. I have no hesitation in recommending him for any appointment requiring a man of ability and integrity. I have never felt, in spite of the great difference in rank, that I must treat him as a non-commissioned officer, but have always been able to treat him as a personal friend. He has served under me for nearly a year. Military Character exemplary.

There was a further excellent report sbout Colin's specific work from the Economic Branch Field Information Agency (Technical), 69 H.Q., C.C.G., B.A.O.R., dated 2 August 1946 and signed by Joan Sinclair. In it she made three points of reference:

1. S/Sgt C.E. Anson has been doing work in this branch as a translator and interpreter since October 1945
2. S/Sgt Anson has been handling highly technical reports dealing with economics and industry, armaments and munitions, metals, engineering, chemicals, etc.
3. S/Sgt Anson's work has been consistently excellent. His translations are always reliable and presented in good English style. This branch has been entirely satisfied with his work.

In Colin's Release Leave Certificate, dated the following day, 3 August 1946, Major Wilson also described his conduct as exemplary and wrote:

Most efficient NCO. Has been employed as an Interpreter for the last year and has given every satisfaction. Far above average intelligence, very popular with all ranks in his unit. Tactful and capable. Highly recommended.

Colin had the opportunity to apply for a commission whilst serving in the Mediterranean but decided that he did not want to sign on for further service, even as an officer. He returned to England to begin life as a civilian again and was demobbed in August 1946.

Civilian Life

here was never any question of Colin going back to Germany to
live permanently. He felt comfortable and at home in England. Having spent a
year in Germany with the British Control Commission, he knew he could never
make Germany his home again: 'I was familiar with the strange upside-down
world of post-war Germany which was totally unnatural. It was not a pleasant
country to settle in. I looked forward to being back in Britain and civilian life.'
In August 1946 Colin returned to Britain and was demobbed. When he arrived
at the release centre, he entered as Sergeant Anson, relinquished his military kit,
was issued with a demob suit and items of clothing, and left as Mr Anson. 'It was
strange,' he comments, 'to be addressed as Mr Anson after being a Private and
Sergeant for so many years.' He immediately took steps to bring his mother out
of Germany to England, but that took time. He continued to correspond for a
while with Livia in Rome even after his discharge from the army. But it was not
going to be possible to sustain the relationship for several reasons:

I had to write and tell her I was not British, technically a German *and* a
refugee. I had neither education nor qualification, nor job or money. I had a
responsibility for my mother in Germany and it was out of the question that we
could take the relationship any further. I was not in a position to take on any
further responsibility. That was the end of our affair. In the long run, it would
not have lasted.

Colin was under no illusions concerning just how difficult it was going to be to settle into civilian life, find employment and earn enough money to support himself. As a refugee whose education had been disrupted under the Hitler regime, finding work would be particularly difficult. He started to write lots of letters to apply for various jobs. He focused on travel companies, particularly airlines; he had always been interested in aeroplanes, and his only qualification was his native language – German. Finally he received a letter from Southampton Air Services at Eastleigh offering him an interview. He was offered the job and agreed the terms:

> I reported at Eastleigh airfield where I was to work as a general factotum, personal assistant to Basil Smailes. It was hard work but I enjoyed it enormously. I did not have much time off at weekends. For example in the Christmas of 1946–7, I took New Year's Day off. The following day when I turned up for work the boss asked, 'Where were you yesterday?' I replied: 'It was New Year's Day.' 'So what?' came the reply. That was a lesson learned, but I liked the job very much and was happy there. Basil Smailes was an easy and friendly man to work for. It was a small air charter Company, financed by a gentleman by the name of Mr Bingham. The airfield had all kinds of aircraft ranging from a Miles Falcon and Stinson Reliant four-seaters to a Lockheed 12 Electra and a Lockheed 18 Lodestar. The mixed bunch of different aircraft, mostly ex-service, was expensive to run because of the number of engineering staff needed who were certified to service the different engines and airframes. But transport was at such a premium after the war, with shipping space booked for years ahead, that it paid so long as the aircraft were flying. On the ground, they were huge white elephants.
>
> It was here that I saw the taxying trials of the Cunliffe-Owen Concordia [not the later Concorde], a feeder airliner, twin engine. The boss arranged a room for my accommodation. It was rather primitive and with a lady I did not get on well with. I was introduced eventually to a lady who had a farmhouse at Sherfield House, Sherfield English, near Romsey. I lived in half the farmhouse, which constituted just a few rooms. When my mother finally immigrated to England that is where we lived.

Colin had already begun to feel British in the commandos, but he was still technically a German. On 28 December 1946, he swore the oath of allegiance and was naturalised as a British citizen. Mrs Ascher left behind her life in Germany to settle in Britain with her son. Colin travelled to Hull and met her off the boat. The first place they visited en route back to Colin's home was the Clelands' house in Liverpool. He wanted to introduce his mother to his adopted family, the family who had acted as his next-of-kin whilst in the commandos. Then he brought her to Sherfield English:

It was wonderful for mother and me to be together again. We had a stable life in a stable country in contrast to Germany. I did not want to live in Germany, although I feel perfectly comfortable to visit there. I have many German friends. I felt my roots were in Britain. And now I was a British subject.

One day, Colin's landlady's sister and husband visited the farmhouse and came with their daughter Pam from London. Colin was introduced to her: 'my eye was caught by Pam's blue eyes.'

Pam took up employment as a secretary to Lord Louis and Lady Edwina Mountbatten at nearby Broadlands. She lived with her aunt at Sherfield House, such that Colin saw a lot of her:

We became close and decided we would get married. Presently, Southampton Air Services collapsed and I had to look for another job. But my time there meant that I had learnt a lot about aviation, acquired people skills and administration experience as personal assistant to the boss. I had a number of jobs for a while, including working on the land at the farm.

Colin then went up to London for interviews and had a succession of jobs which did not last long and were unsuccessful. Then he took up employment with Hotel Plan which was much more successful. Hotel Plan was a travel company based in Switzerland, with an office in London. They introduced the idea of package holidays and Colin spent his time building up the air charter part of their package holiday business:

I also travelled when a courier couldn't do a certain job, and accompanied small groups by train to Switzerland. At other times I began building up the air travel business which proved successful. It was an interesting time.

It was during this period that Colin met an old friend, Peter Bliss, from the Pioneer Corps days. Peter had been discharged from the army for medical reasons, but beforehand they had been good friends in 87 Company Pioneer Corps. Peter had then worked for a while for the Americans. Now, post-war, he was working for Poly Travel, at the northern end of Regent Street, not far from where Colin worked for Hotel Plan near Oxford Circus. They first met after the war when Peter called into the offices where Colin was to discuss travel matters. They started to socialise together after work and went to cafes for coffee. Peter was instrumental in introducing Colin to his future wife Alice. He recalls:

I was still seeing Pam who was working at Broadlands whenever I could. I was now living with my mother in Willesden Green, north-west London. The relationship with Pam became rather strained and in spring 1948 it came to a head and we split up. That was rather a heartbreak for me and affected me for eighteen months. Peter Bliss was a wonderful friend to me during that period and helped me through. We were having coffee one day when Peter spotted someone he knew and waved. He left me at the table and went over to say hello to them. It was Alice with her mother. Peter had been with the British Expeditionary Force in France and rumoured killed at Dunkirk, but in fact had got back via Brest. So Alice's mother was taken aback to see him and then told him that Alice's father had died. She had re-married and was living in Temple Fortune, north-west London. Peter told them that he would introduce me properly one day, which he did when he took me to the house in Finchley which Alice shared with her brother Bill. Alice and I became friends. I tended to miss the last 660 Trolley Bus which took me from Willesden Green to Finchley Central! It was a happy friendship, not a mad love affair to begin with. We went out together, for example, the Festival of Britain, and had a truly wonderful day together. We began to realise that we would like to spend the rest of our lives together. It wasn't long after that that we got engaged with the blessing of both families.

Alice was also a refugee from Nazi oppression. She was born Alice Gross in Vienna in September 1924 to Otto and Edith Gross. Her father, director of a bank in Vienna in the 1920s, had served in the Austro-Hungarian Army in the First World War and been decorated for bravery. Her grandfather owned a factory making pipes and smokers' requisites, and also acted as Austrian agent for Dunhill. He had many business friends in Great Britain. The situation deteriorated for Austria's Jews immediately after Adolf Hitler annexed the country in March 1938. Alice and her family survived, aware that things were getting steadily worse. There was no future for them in Vienna, little knowing then that Hitler's persecution of Jews would eventually lead to the Final Solution and complete annihilation. In October 1938 Alice left Vienna to stay with some of her grandfather's friends in England. Fortunately she had already left by the time the Nazis unleashed *Kristallnacht* on 9–10 November that year. In February 1939, her parents followed to England, escaping via Czechoslovakia which had not yet been annexed by Hitler. Alice's brother Bill stayed with some of their grandfather's friends in England, trained as an engineer and was employed as such during the war. After the war he moved to Canada and finally America.

Living first in Coulsdon in Surrey, Alice was treated as a member of the host family. She helped with the children and carried out household duties. Nine months later war had broken out and she moved into the house shared by her parents with her aunt and uncle in Central Finchley, a house which later became her parents' permanent home. Eventually she was apprenticed as a dressmaker to Debenham & Freebody in Wigmore Street for about two years. Soon after the outbreak of war, the company changed from dressmaking to essential war work making army uniforms. Alice recalls: 'I made straps for the belts in the army battledress trousers for a year and a half.' She then took up a job with a dressmaker in South Kensington before moving to The White House in Bond Street, a high class dress and lingerie shop, as a dressmaker.

Alice volunteered for the forces and in March 1943 her call-up papers finally arrived. She was accepted for the Women's Auxiliary Air Force (WAAF), a rare posting for an Austrian national. She became one of only a few refugee women to serve in the WAAF, the majority having been with the Auxiliary Territorial Service (ATS). Alice had an extremely interesting job in the WAAF.

I was sent to Innsworth, Gloucestershire where I was kitted out with my uniform. I learnt marching and drill. After four weeks everyone received their posting. I wanted to be a driver but there were no vacancies so I was assigned as a clerk. I was eventually sent to Madeley in Herefordshire, a training camp for aircrew signals with over 800 men and 100 women. We were billeted in Nissen huts on a WAAF site. I worked in the office, routing people. So for example, if someone failed their exams I completed the paperwork for them to return to unit (RTU). I also organised all the travel warrants.

After about eight months I asked to be re-mustered for training as a photographer. I was posted to No.1 School of Photography at Farnborough, Hants for twelve weeks of training with exams every week. At the end of the training I was graded LACW – leading aircraft woman, a better result than I had dared hoped for. From Farnborough I was posted to RAF Croydon, where we were billeted in private houses. We spent all our nights sleeping in the Morrison shelter because of the bombing raids, and constantly wore steel helmets due to the start of the V-1 bombardment, one of the first of which landed in Croydon. From there I was posted to RAF Gatwick. The headquarters building was known as the beehive because it looked like one, and is now a listed building outside the Gatwick Airport area. My duties consisted of helping the dentist because there was no photographic section on the base.

From Gatwick, she was posted to HQ Bomber Command at High Wycombe which had an underground photographic section. There she was responsible for processing the five-inch-wide film strips which came in from the bomber target cameras. Once developed and printed, the photographs were taken next door to the photographic interpreters. She recalls:

Sometimes they came back to us for enlargement depending on what the interpreters had seen on the image. On one particular occasion, a photo was sent back to us and a section of it marked about the size of a postage stamp. We were asked to enlarge just that area. We had to photograph it using glass plates in those days and enlarge it to twenty inches by sixteen. This was then sent back to the interpreters and that was how we found where the V-1 flying bombs were launched in northern France.

From High Wycombe Alice was sent to Sturgate, Lincolnshire, again attached to Bomber Command and carrying out printing and developing work. It was here that F24 cameras were attached to the aircraft and their films came back to their unit for developing.

Alice's wartime service was not limited to Britain. She volunteered for active service overseas and in March 1946 landed at Heliopolis in Egypt. She travelled to her next base, RAF Ismailia, where she carried out photographic duties and then to work station 107 MU. Later she was posted to RAF Deversoir with three other photographers, working in an office of the Warrant Officer alongside German POWs who were happy to be doing congenial work and were well looked after. There she was engaged in taking photographs for the military authorities of important events, such as parades, or the funeral of an ATS woman killed by an insurgent bomb. Alice was demobilised at Christmas 1946–47 and returned to Finchley, north-west London. After the war she worked for a society photographer covering social events and magazines like *The Tatler*. During her time with them, she took official photographs at the silver wedding anniversary of the then duke and duchess of Norfolk, and at a tea given by Mrs Atlee at 10 Downing Street, amongst other events.

Colin and Alice married on 21 December 1951. On 5 December 1953 their first child Barbara Hedda Anson was born; followed by Diana Judith on 1 March 1955, and Edward Henry on 13 February 1958. They have seven grandchildren. Once the children were at school Alice kept busy running a launderette and soon discovered that her strengths lay with people. This led to years of dedicated work with many charitable organisations including Gingerbread, conceiving of and setting up a furniture scheme for families on benefits, setting up and running local holiday play schemes to help single-parent families, then twenty years with Women's Refuge. In latter years she devoted her time to working for the Rape Crisis and Sexual Abuse Centre in Hertfordshire and the ORT charity shop in Finchley.

The job at the travel firm Hotel Plan came to an end. Colin's friend Peter Bliss introduced him to his uncle who ran a small engineering company in Kilburn. Colin became his secretary and factotum for about three years. Then he spent about a year selling *Encyclopaedia Britannica* door-to-door. There was a period selling point-of-sale advertising ideas, which did not prove a great success, and this was followed by a year at Remington Rand, selling filing systems. But then Colin was employed by his father-in-law Henry's company as a salesman, 'again not with any startling success,' he says.

> But when my mother was granted a fairly generous sum and pension under the German Restitution legislation, she enabled me to set up as a manufacturer of paper shredding machines, and other engineering products, in partnership with my father-in-law. Again, it was not a huge success, but it provided plenty of variegated experience. Eventually, I sold the production business and became a part of Henry's very successful motor accessory group. That is where my small company created its own niche, such that life and work settled on a solid basis, later working for Henry's younger son Gordon, culminating in a happy and comfortable retirement in 1986.

When not at work, one central hobby dominated Colin's life and had to do with planes:

> Already when I was a schoolboy in Germany, the newsreels showed daring young men teetering off the sand dunes of Rossitten on the Baltic coast, and the Wasserkuppe in the Rön Mountains in central Germany, on simple open-framed training gliders. The elegance in cutting-edge sailplanes of that time, still with wooden wing spars and ribs, plywood planking and even doped fabric, developed aircraft of up to thirty-metre wingspan. The poetic magic of seeing them against a bright sky with the translucent wings showing all the filigree of the woodwork inside was magic to me. I would love to have been part of all that but in the 1930s, I did not have the opportunity and I was too young. Something stuck, and remained encapsulated in my heart. My interest in planes was general and I began to read quite technical books on aircraft and aero-engine development and the military aircraft fleets of the totalitarian regimes.

Then one chance stop during a journey to Scotland on a family holiday changed the course of Colin's life. They had often gone camping but now they had upgraded to caravans, having enjoyed a caravanning holiday in Austria. One hot summer they decided to take their caravan to Scotland. They were late leaving and only got as far as a campsite at Dunstable Downs in Bedfordshire. They parked up and Colin soon realised they were on the edge of an airfield:

> I looked up at the glider overhead. Flying was the great desire of my youth and something stirred in my heart. We decided to go and have a closer look. We had a friendly welcome and were invited to watch the gliders taking off in a westerly

direction below the downs. We walked across the field towards the launch point. It was a long way, so I decided to go back and collect the car. A friendly man Peter stopped and asked me if I wanted a lift back to the Clubhouse to get my car. I gratefully accepted. The he asked whether I would like a flight. I brought the car back to launch point and Peter was already there. He gave me a flight in K13, a two-seater. It really grabbed me. The flight was followed by tea with Peter and his wife in their caravan before we carried on our holiday to Scotland. But somehow this incident would not let me go and kept nagging at me. After we had returned from our holiday, I made the mistake of going back to Dunstable to look at the planes again. The desire to fly burst open in my heart and I knew I had to learn. The desire became feverish and chronic.

That day whilst I was standing at launch point watching the gliders take off, the instructor turned around and said: 'would you mind, we're a bit thin on the ground. This is signal bat.' He showed me signals. 'Now', he said, 'would you like to do this for me?' It was more a statement. I was caught; I was part of it all. There was no turning back. I said to someone nearby that I would really like another flight. He said – why waste your money on another passenger flight? Why don't you join now and make that your first proper lesson? When I returned home to Alice that day I had a very sheepish face and Alice knew immediately what had happened. That was my beginning of gliding life at the London Gliding Club. It took fifteen months for me to fly solo. That's a long time and at times it felt it, but then I was already fifty-one years old at the time. Most people start younger.

When Colin finally went solo in December 1974, he realised it was only the beginning of learning to fly properly. He began to take gliding very seriously and it became a way of life rather than an intermittent hobby. Alice agreed that he could fly on Saturdays as long as he spent Sundays with the family. Eventually Alice accompanied him to the airfield, although she never flew a glider herself, and they became friendly with other members of the Club. Colin flew two-seater vintage gliders, one of which he part-owned, as well as owning shares in more modern machines. The Club became a family of friends. They flew at different clubs in Britain and Colin also became a flying instructor. On one occasion Colin's path crossed with the prolific romantic novelist, the late Barbara Cartland, as he explains:

The open-cockpit vintage two-seater was popular with photographers and for filming, for the unobstructed field of view from the front cockpit. On one occasion, it stood in for an old type, no longer available, which had been used to try out an idea which Barbara Cartland tried to introduce: a mail distribution system by means of a train of gliders, towed by a powered aircraft, with the gliders dropping off at various destinations to deliver their cargo of mailbags. In April 1985, the Noel Edmonds serial *The Time of your Life* featured Barbara Cartland, and our glider was temporarily decorated to look like the BAC 7 glider with her name on the side. We had a lovely day's flying at Hatfield to re-create the 1930s trial flight in which mail bags had been delivered from Maidstone in Kent to a meadow outside Reading, where the glider landed to hand them over to the Mayor and Corporation awaiting it.

Colin was drawn to vintage gliders and became a member of the Vintage Glider Club. He took part in Vintage Glider Rallies, which he says 'have a particular charm of their own'. It was then that he and Alice established an international worldwide family of friends. The members flew each others' different types of aircraft and became a close-knit community who met once a year at the international rally. The rallies were held in a different country annually. Beforehand members usually spent a week to ten days at a different location in that country as a holiday. Colin and Alice structured their holidays around the international rallies. In 1995 the rally was at Oberschleissheim, outside Munich in Germany:

> It was an old airfield of the Bavarian Royal Flying Corps before the First World War. During that rally we flew over Munich which was wonderful. But there was one thing which was very odd for me to deal with psychologically. I flew over the former concentration camp at Dachau, just north of Oberschleissheim. Flying over that grisly rectangle in which my father suffered and died, whilst having a lovely time enjoying myself as a pilot, was a strangely schizophrenic experience. A couple days later, Alice and I visited Dachau, now a museum. It felt emotionally strangely neutral, almost sanitized. I thought I would feel something standing there in the camp itself, but I didn't. It was rather sterile. It was a strange sensation. I did not want to find out precisely how my father died there. I don't ever want to know the painful details.

At the end of the flying season of the summer of 1997, when Colin was seventy-five, he decided not to renew his basic instructor rating. Gradually he was less and less in current practice as a pilot and decided it was time to stop within a few years. He felt greatly honoured when his gliding career was crowned by his being made President of the London Gliding Club.

Colin was ever conscious of his part in the war with the commandos and over the years attended a number of reunions of the Commando Association at the Seymour Hall in London. Due to dwindling numbers, the association has now disbanded. In 1952 a statue memorial of three commando figures with the motto

'United we Conquer' was unveiled at Spean Bridge near Achnacarry in Scotland. Colin was amongst 300 commandos well enough to travel to Scotland for the ceremony, where the green berets received the freedom of Lochaber. Members of 3 Troop have had their own reunions too. The first, organised by Colin, was held in Eastbourne in 1984 and attended by members from all over the world. On 1 May 1999, Colin along with other comrades attended the unveiling of a special memorial to 3 Troop at Aberdovery (Aberdyfi) in North Wales where they had trained (see photo 33). It was their last troop reunion.

In 2007, after the publication of *The King's Most Loyal Enemy Aliens* by the author, media attention turned for the first time to the story of the refugees who served in the British forces during the Second World War. It was a relatively unknown story in the public domain. In September 2007, over 250 veterans and their relatives gathered at the Imperial War Museum, London, for the first ever reunion of the refugees from Nazism who fought for Britain. Field Marshal Lord Bramall gave the opening address, followed by five veteran speeches. In his speech, Lord Bramall paid tribute to the bravery of these men and women and remembered those who did not return from the theatre of war, amongst them heavy losses from 3 Troop:

> I know that you will all have memories of the extraordinary comradeship which develops between soldiers, but that these of course are tinged with great regret at the loss of many promising young lives. And so we remember also today those of your comrades who did not come back: those who fell in battle or who, having been dropped behind enemy lines, were ambushed, captured and killed. The campaign which followed the Normandy landings saw thousands killed in action, and many who should rightfully be here today lost their lives at that crucial time. And then there were numerous special missions – both secret and dangerous – for which your comrades laid down their lives.

Colin was one of the five veterans who spoke that day, he on behalf of 3 Troop. He gave some poignant reflections on his own wartime service with the commandos. In early 2009, Colin and Alice were interviewed for a documentary entitled *Churchill's German Army*, first screened on the National Geographic Channel on 26 April. Interest in the media continues with that subject and Colin is sometimes interviewed by the press about his time in the commandos.

CHAPTER 11

Postscript

I t is seventy years since Colin first arrived in Britain as a refugee from Nazi Germany. Now in his late eighties he is ever mindful of his roots and the debt he owes to Britain for saving his life. 'My mother was thrilled that I had fought for Britain,' he says. 'But I often think of my father, even after all these years. I admired him greatly and miss him tremendously.' In serving in the British Commandos in the war, Colin has given something back to the country that offered him refuge. How does he feel towards Germany? The answer to that question is aptly demonstrated by an incident which happened to him just a few years ago whilst travelling by train through Austria with his wife Alice:

In our carriage there was an older man with young boy. It turned out to be grandfather and grandson. The grandfather was explaining in German about the mountains we were passing through. Alice and I found it very interesting and started to join the conversation in German. Then we talked about holidays, different countries and travel. He said that he had been in Sicily. And I replied: 'Yes, me too, but that was only during the war.' He then said, 'Ah, I was in the Luftwaffe, a Stuka pilot.' I was surprised and admitted that I had been hit by a Stuka. One thing led to another and it transpired that he remembered an operation over Sicily in which he and his mates had had to attack Allied shipping in Augusta Bay. His memory was so accurate: 'But,' he said, 'a smokescreen had been laid and obscured most of the ships – with the exception of one, so we concentrated our fire on that one ship that was laying the smoke screen.' It was the moment when I realised that he may well be the very pilot who had dropped the bomb that wounded me! He was terribly embarrassed and I had to console him and explain: Why should I resent it? It was his job. It was his duty. Today I would not hold it against anyone for having been a Nazi. What else should they have done?

Alice and I always feel perfectly happy in Germany, especially now. The current generation are not Nazis and have no personal link to the actions of the Nazi regime. They are not responsible for the actions of their ancestors. They often feel guilt by association for what their parents or grandparents may have done during the war.

Remembrance for a veteran who has lived through so much and served in the elite commandos is important. Every Armistice Day, Colin and Alice make a point of watching on TV the annual service from the Royal Albert Hall, London. After seven decades, it still has the power to move him:

> The ceremony is rather lengthy, but at the end, in that moment of silence when the petals descend from the dome, they are all there: I see their faces. My comrades who died fighting for Britain. I see Robbie, Ernest and Eric, and Mac. And that gets me every time and chokes me to tears.

Whilst finishing this book, I was reminded of a quote by Edmund Burke, which for me sums up Colin's sacrifice for the country that saved him:

> All that is necessary for evil to triumph is for good men to do nothing.

Colin Anson, like 10,000 other German refugees, did not sit back and do nothing. The British government could not conscript them into the forces because they were of enemy nationality. Colin, like 10,000 other German and Austrian refugees, volunteered to fight for his adopted country. Given what Colin and his family had suffered in Germany, and having got out with his life, he could have taken a different path of self-preservation. He could have left it to others, but didn't. It was simply not an option for him. This was his war and he was determined to play his part in the defeat of Nazism. He and his comrades of 3 Troop put their lives on the line, in extraordinarily dangerous missions, so that future generations might live in freedom. Curt Ascher would have been very proud of his son.

Appendix 1

Nominal Roll of 3 Troop 10 Commando Personnel Attached to 2 Commando Brigade, CMF

OFFICERS

Lieut. Bartlett, K W	The Buffs
Lieut. Shelley, A	Royal Marines
Lieut. Stewart, D	Royal Marines

OTHER RANKS

Pte Anderson. A	Royal West Kents
L.Sgt. Anson C	Royal Sussex
Fus. Burnett, W R	Royal Fusiliers
Cfn. Foster, R	REME
Pte Gray, F	Royal West Kents
Cpl. Hudson, S K	Hampshire
Pte. Martin, W	Royal West Kents
Pte Minas, E	OHLI
Pte Peters, H R	Black Watch
L/Cpl. Ross, S	Buffs

Pte. Scott, J	Royal West Kents
Pte. Smith, J	Lincs
Dvr. Spielman, D. W	RASC
Pte. Stevens, T	Royal West Kents
Pte. Stewart, J	Royal West Kents
Cfn. Ward, G	REME
Pte. Warren, H	Royal West Kents
Pte. Warwick, R D	Essex
Pte. White, A	Royal West Kents

Appendix 2

3 TROOP TRAINING PROGRAMMES

Sunday 25.02.45–Saturday 03.03.45

SUNDAY

Cross-country and road march (25 miles)

MONDAY

Morning		**Afternoon**	
0830–0920	Drill	1330–1430	Weapons training
0930–1030	Map reading	1430–1510	Use of compass
1040–1100	Physical training	1510–1710	Rifle range
1110–1210	Map reading		

TUESDAY

Morning		**Afternoon**	
0830–0920	Drill	1330–1710	Compass march
0930–1000	Physical training		
1010–1210	Range (Bren)		

WEDNESDAY _____

Admin Day (Valley of Death)

THURSDAY _____

Morning		**Afternoon**	
0830–0920	Drill	1330–1710	Road march
0930–1020	Weapons training		
1030–1100	Unarmed combat		
1110–1210	Map reading		

FRIDAY _____

Map reading and fieldcraft

SATURDAY _____

Morning		**Afternoon**	
0830–0920	Drill	1330–1430	Weapons training
0930–1000	Physical training	1445–1710	Range
1010–1130	Speed march	2000–2230	Night compass march
1130–1210	Weapons training – Quiz		

Monday 5.03.45–Saturday 10.03.45

MONDAY _____

Morning		**Afternoon**	
0830–0910	Drill	1330–1455	Weapons training (Colt)
0915–1040	Weapons training (36 grenade)	1500–1710	Range (zeroing rifles)
1045–1125	Physical training	2000	Night observation,
1130–1210	Weapons training (Bren)		compass march

TUESDAY

Morning		**Afternoon**	
0830–0910	Drill	1330–1410	Weapons training (69 grenade)
0915–1040	Weapons training (36 grenade)	1415–1710	Range (36 & 69 grenades)
1045–1125	Physical training		
1130–1210	Weapons, Colt		

WEDNESDAY

24 hour scheme: map reading by day and night, orientation

THURSDAY

Morning	**Afternoon**	
Compulsory rest	1330–1455	Weapons training (Colt)
	1500–1545	Physical training

FRIDAY

Fieldcraft, Andria areas   Andria range

SATURDAY

Morning		**Afternoon**	
0830–0910	Drill	1330–1540	Range (Colt, TMC)
0915–1040	2" mortar	1545–1710	Speed march
1045–1125	Physical training		
1130–1210	Weapons training (Colt)		

Monday 12.03.45–Saturday 17.03.45

MONDAY

Morning		**Afternoon**	
0830–0910	Drill	1330–1710	Battle drill, attacks
0915–1040	Section movement & attack		
1045–1125	Weapons training (2" mortar)		
1130–1210	Physical training		

TUESDAY _____

Morning		**Afternoon**	
0830–0910	Physical training	1330–1710	Weapons training (Colt, grenades 36, 69, 77)
0915–1040	Defence		
1040–1210	Weapons training	2000	Night visibility, listening exercise

WEDNESDAY _____

Morning		**Afternoon**	
0830–1210	Open range	1330–1710	Fieldcraft & battle drill

THURSDAY _____

All day map reading scheme

FRIDAY _____

Morning		**Afternoon**	
0830–1210	Battle drill	1330–1410	Drill
		1415–1710	Range (Bren, TMC, Colt)
		2000	Night map reading scheme

SATURDAY _____

Morning		**Afternoon**	
0830–0910	Drill	1330–1540	House clearing
0915–0955	Physical training	1545–1710	Speed march
1000–1210	Street fighting		

Monday 19.03.45–Saturday 24.03.45

MONDAY _____

Morning		**Afternoon**	
0830–0910	PT	1330–1540	Weapons training (Karabiner 98, MG 34 & 42)
0915–0955	WT Sten		
1000–1040	Drill		

| 1045–1210 | Demolition | 1545–1710 | Recce patrols & patrol reports |
| | | 2000 | Night map reading |

TUESDAY _____

Morning		**Afternoon**	
0830–0910	Drill	1330–1710	Ambush & infiltration exercises
0915–1040	Demolition		
1045–1125	Physical training		
1130–1210	Ambush		

WEDNESDAY _____

36 hours scheme: map reading, infiltration, patrols, sleeping out

THURSDAY _____

| **Morning** | **Afternoon** | |
| 36 hours scheme continued, | 1330–1710 | Night patrols, lecture & drill |

FRIDAY _____

Morning		**Afternoon**	
0830–0955	Mines	1330–1710	Valley of Death (Bren TMC, Colt, 36 grenades
1000–1040	MG 34 &42	1045–1125	Drill
1130–1210	Physical training		

SATURDAY _____

Morning		**Afternoon**	
0830–1040	Mines	1330–1710	Exercise "ME"
1045–1210	WT: Machine-Carbine 38		

Notes

1. The assassination was fourteen years to the day that Franz Ferdinand had put his signature to a Declaration of Renunciation of Succession Rights, signing away the rights of their children to succeed to the throne on his death.
2. The Schlieffen Plan was devised in 1895 by Count Alfred von Schlieffen (1833–1913) on which German strategy was unsuccessfully based in World War I. In the event of a German war on two fronts, he envisaged a German breakthrough in Belgium and the defeat of France within six weeks by a colossal right-wheel flanking movement through Holland and then southwards, cutting off Paris from the sea, meanwhile holding off any Russian intervention with a smaller army in the east. In fact Holland was not invaded during the war and remained neutral throughout.
3. Michiel Adriaanszoon de Ruyter (1607-76), Dutch Naval Commander, who became an admiral in the Dutch Navy. He served with distinction in the first Anglo-Dutch War (1652-54). In the second Anglo-Dutch War (1665-67) he famously sailed up the River Medway, burned some of the English ships, and then sailed up the River Thames, as well as attacking Harwich.
4. See Helen Fry, *Music and Men: The Life & Loves of Harriet Cohen*.
5. Claus believes that this refers to the amount payable to the Court under a legal judgement to pay off debts after the financial crash.
6. Dated 21 December 1938.
7. Letter date 20 December 1938.

8. Certificate dated 16 December 1938.
9. Letter dated 2 February 1939.
10. For a background to Kitchener Camp, see Helen Fry, *Jews in North Devon during the Second World War*; Harry Rossney, *Grey Dawns*; Norman Bentwich, *I understand the Risks*; and Amy Gottlieb, *Men of Vision: Anglo-Jewry's Aid to Victims of the Nazi Regime*.
11. Letter dated 14 November 1939.
12. Letter dated 19 October 1940, sent from Wallingford.
13. For a full history see Helen Fry, *The King's Most Loyal Enemy Aliens*, published in paperback as *Churchill's German Army*; Norman Bentwich, *I Understand the Risks*; and Peter Leighton-Langer, *The King's Own Loyal Enemy Aliens*.
14. See Helen Fry, *Jews in North Devon during the Second World War*.
15. For a fuller biography of Martin Freud's service in the Pioneer Corps see the relevant chapters in Helen Fry, *Freuds' War*.
16. For a profile of Arthur Koestler in the British army, see *Jews in North Devon*, op. cit.
17. Their extraordinary achievements are charted in detail with photographs and illustrations in *Jews in North Devon*, chapter 5.
18. For a background history, see Harry Rossney, *Grey Dawns* and Helen Fry, *The King's Most Loyal Enemy Aliens*.
19. For detailed profiles of men in the special forces, see Helen Fry, *The King's Most Loyal Enemy Aliens*.
20. See Helen Fry, *Freuds' War* and Anton Walter Freud's unpublished memoirs *Before the Anticlimax*.
21. Garry Rogers, *Interesting Times*, pp. 124–5.
22. Ref: E. Coll. Grave 16b–16r.
23. For more on Anton Walter Freud, see *Freuds' War*, op.cit.
24. One such decoy was the corpse of Major Martin (the man who never was) planted with convincing data about his 'body' to lure the Germans to the East Mediterranean.
25. A 35,000 ton battle-ship (ex-Jellicoe, renamed February 1940).
26. SV = synthetic vibram.
27. For fuller details, see Peter Masters, *Striking Back* and Ian Dear, *Ten Commando*.
28. A colour copy of these two paintings now exists in the archives of the Imperial War Museum, London.
29. *Soldier*, The British Army Magazine, 8 December 1945, p. 5.
30. This is taken from St Paul's letter to the Romans 12 v. 19 which is quoting Deut. 32 v. 35.

Selected Bibliography

PAPERS AND ARCHIVES

Documents collection and the Sound Archive at The Imperial War Museum; The Association of Jewish Ex-service Men and Women (AJEX); The Association of Jewish Refugees; The Public Record Office, Kew. Official war diaries of 40 (RM) Commando, ref: DEFE 2/48; war diaires of No. 10. Inter-Allied Commando, ref: WO 218/40; Brian Hilton-Jones report on 3 Troop, ref: DEFE 2/977. Copies of the newspapers *Vis of the World* and *Vis-à-Vis*, newspaper archives of The Imperial War Museum. *Soldier*, The British Army Magazine, 8 December 1945, copy in Colin Anson's papers.

BOOKS AND MEMOIRS

Ambrose, Tom. *Hitler's Loss: What Britain and America gained from Europe's cultural exiles*, Peter Owen: 2001
Bender, Edgar. *Reminiscenes of the Pioneer Corps: 1940-1942*, unpublished
Bentwich, Norman. *I Understand the Risks: The Story of the Refugees from Nazi Oppression who Fought in the British Forces in the World War*, Victor Gollancz: 1950
Berghahn, Marion. *Continental Britons: German-Jewish Refugees from Nazi Germany*, Berg Publishers: 1988
Cresswell, Yvonne. *Living With the Wire: Civilian Internment in the Isle of Man during the two World Wars*, Manx National Heritage: 1994
Dear, Ian. *Ten Commando 1942-1945*, Leo Cooper: 1987

Dunning, James. *It Had to Be Tough. The fascinating story of the origins of the Commandos and their special training in World War II*, The Pentland Press: 2000

Fry, Helen. *Denazification*, The History Press: 2010

Fry, Helen. *Churchill's German Army*, The History Press: 2009

Fry, Helen. *Freuds' War*, The History Press: 2009

Fry, Helen. *From Dachau to D-Day*, The History Press: 2009

Fry, Helen. *Music and Men: The Life & Loves of Harriet Cohen*, The History Press: 2008

Fry, Helen. *The King's Most Loyal Enemy Aliens: Germans who Fought for Britain during the Second World War*, Sutton: 2007

Fry, Helen. *Jews in North Devon during the Second World War*, Halsgrove: 2005

Gillman, Peter & Gillman, Leni. *Collar the Lot: How Britain Interned and Expelled its Wartime Refugees*, Quartet Books: 1980

Gottlieb, Amy Zahl. *Men of Vision: Anglo-Jewry's Aid to Victims of the Nazi Regime 1933-1945*, Weidenfeld & Nicolson: 1998

Grenville, Anthony. *Continental Britons: Jewish Refugees from Nazi Europe*, The Jewish Museum, London: 2002

Hampshire, A. Cecil. *Beachhead Commandos*, William Kimber: 1983

Leighton–Langer, Peter. *X Steht für unbekannt: Deutsche und Österreicher in den Britischen Streitkräften im Zweiten Weltkrieg* ("X Means Unknown: Germans and Austrians in the British Fighting Forces in the Second World War"), Verlag, Berlin: 1999

Leighton–Langer, Peter. *The King's Own Loyal Enemy Aliens*, Vallentine Mitchell: 2006

Masters, Peter. *Striking Back: A Jewish Commandos War Against the Nazis*, Presidio Press: 1997

Mitchell, Raymond. *Marine Commando: Sicily and Salerno, 1943 with 41 Royal Marines Commando*, Hale: 1988

Perry, Geoffrey. *When Life Becomes History*, White Mountain Press: 2002

Rogers, Garry. *Interesting Times*, privately published autobiography: 1998

Rossney, Harry. *Grey Dawns: Illustrated Poems about Life in Nazi Germany, Emigration, and Active Service in the British Army during the War*, History Web: 2009

Rothman, Herman. *Hitler's Will* (ed. Helen Fry), The History Press: 2009

Stent, Ronald. *A Bespattered Page? The Internment of 'His Majesty's most Loyal Enemy Aliens'*, Andre Deutsch: 1980

Sugarman, Martin. *No 3 (Jewish) Troop, No. 10 Commando*, privately published paper, copy given to the author

Young, D. *Four Five*, Leo Cooper Ltd: 1972

Index

Abbassia 109

Aberdovey 74, 80–88

Achnacarry 75–88, 135, 168

Albania (raids on) 11, 119–28, 131, 134

Alexandria 108, 109, 111

Amadeus Quartet 52

America 28, 41, 43, 46, 53, 59, 67, 118, 162

Anderson Manor 63

Andria, plain of (Italy) 135, 175

Anson, Alice (née Gross) 74, 161–64, 166, 167, 169, 170

Ascher, Curt 13, 15–23, 29, 32, 35–40, 153, 170

Ascher, Mathilde 13, 19, 20, 23, 36–39, 42, 43, 45–47, 53, 54, 59, 62, 95, 136, 149, 151, 153, 155, 159–62, 165, 169

Augusta Bay 98, 169

Austria 15, 40, 58, 125, 165, 169

Auxiliary Military Pioneer Corps
    see Pioneer Corps

Bad Homburg 20–23, 42, 53, 68

BAOR
    see British Army of the Rhine

Barnes, Robert
    (Gotthard, Baumwollspinner) 144

Bartlett, Kenneth (Karl Walter Billman) 74, 81, 84, 103, 105, 108, 135, 142, 148, 151

Baumwollspinner, Gotthard
    see Robert Barnes

Belgium 15, 51, 118, 141

Berlin 13, 15, 16, 18–20, 22, 29, 51, 74, 103, 106, 141, 152–53

Bibelkreis 33

Billman, Karl Walter (see also Kenneth Bartlett) 64, 67, 74

Blackheath (S. London) 59, 60

Blaschke, Mr 47

Bliss, Peter 161, 162, 164

Bökelmann, Dr 13

Brač, island of 115–19

Breiden, Heinz 22

Bremen 19, 23, 35, 39, 150

Breslau 14, 58
British Army of the Rhine (BAOR)
    145, 156
British Control Commission
    see Control Commission

Cairo 102, 104, 105, 107–09
Canadian Field Hospital 95–97
Cape Passero 93
Cartland, Barbara 166–67
Catania 98
Churchill, Jack 117, 121
Churchill, Randolph 114
Churchill, Brigadier Tom 121
Churchill, Winston 52, 73, 142
Cleland family 62, 68, 70, 143, 160
Cleland, Pat 62, 70, 134
Cohen, Harriet 22, 179
Coles, Jean 58
Coles, Lt Col. 58
Commacchio, valley of 138
Commando training 73–90
Commandos
    No. 2 Commando Brigade 7, 109,
    119 ,122, 124–25, 134
    No. 10 Inter-Allied Commando
    73, 83, 143, 155, 181
    3 Troop 70, 73–91, 103, 105, 110, 118,
    119, 135, 137, 144–45, 168, 170, 171,
    173–77
    raising a half-troop in Italy 135
    See Royal Marine Commando
Communists 37, 44, 134
Control Commission 145, 147, 151, 159
Corfu 11, 131-45

D-Day 88, 89, 92, 105, 114, 118, 143, 144
Dachau 37–40, 53, 153, 167
Davies, Jack 144
Devonshire (troopship) 91, 92

Eastbourne 103, 168
Edmonds, Noel 167
Emigration 45–55, 153
Emmerich 47
Ephraims, Capt. 91, 110

Field Intelligence Agency Technical
    (FIAT) 147, 151–52, 156
First World War 15–18, 23, 27, 28, 40, 42,
    46, 49, 97, 162, 167
Frankfurt 19, 21–23, 29, 30-41, 43, 45–
    47, 53, 147–57
Franklin, Mac 84, 86, 91, 105
Freud, (Anton) Walter 63, 67
Füsse im Feuer, Die (poem) 33, 152, 154

Geneifa 104, 106-07, 109
Gerlach, Dr 30
Germany 13–25, 27–43, 47, 49, 50, 54,
    55, 141, 144, 145, 147–57, 159, 161,
    165, 167, 169, 170
    post-war Germany 147–58
Gestapo 12, 32, 37–38, 44, 45, 153
Gliding 166–67
Glatz 14, 37
Goedeke, Leberecht 22
Goering, Hermann 32
Grant, Brian 110
Greenock 91
Gross, Alice
    see Alice Anson

Hamel, Albert 33–34, 152, 154
Harris, Ian (Hans Hajos) 73–74, 144
Helt, Gerhard 132
Henkel, Herr 153–54
Hilton-Jones, Capt. Brian 68–70, 73, 74, 76,
    79, 80, 81, 83, 86, 88, 105, 144, 155, 181
Hitler, Adolf 25, 27, 28, 31, 37, 40, 50, 51,
    53, 89, 141, 162

HMS *Tormentor* 87, 88
Holland 16, 47–48, 141
Hvar, island of 114

Ilfracombe 55, 57–59
Imperial War Museum 168
Isle of Wight 88, 143
Italy 89, 91–110, 120, 125, 127, 132, 135–44

Jerusalem 106
Jupp, Capt. 111, 113, 116

Kapp Putsch 20
Kendal, 'Nobby' (Knobloch) 84, 85,
    109–11, 113, 119, 120
Kindertransport 46
Kitchener Camp 50, 59, 180
Koelz, Johannes Mattheus 58
Koestler, Arthur 58, 180
Komiža 112–13, 117
Kristallnacht 37, 40–42, 162
Kulturbund Orchestra 41

Laddy, Max (Max Lewinsky) 144
Lane, George (Georg Lanyi) 144
Lawrence, Ernie 85, 144
Laycock, Major General 92, 143
Lenzewski, Gustav 21, 151
Lenzewski Quartet 21
Lister, Colonel 84
Liverpool 52, 61–64, 68, 70, 134, 143, 160
Lovat, Lord 77

Masters, Peter (Peter Arany) 180, 182
Maxwell, Robert 58
Mendelssohn, Felix Robert 41
Mendelssohn Quartet 41
Miles, Hugh (Levin) 91, 110, 111
Ministry of Weapons and Equipment
    (Germany) 152

Monopoli 112, 120, 135
Munich 31, 37, 40, 64, 167
Munich Agreement 40
Musch, Hanne 58

Naples 111–12, 120, 142
Neher, Robert 132
Normandy 63, 89, 92, 114, 118, 144, 168
North Africa 33, 63, 100, 143
Noske, Gustav 17–19, 29, 30, 35

O'Neill, Sgt Major 77, 144
Oberschleissheim 167
Operation Husky 92

Pachino 93, 96–97
Palestine 28, 106
Pariser, Mrs 42, 53
Partisans 11, 114–16, 118, 119, 124, 125,
    128–29, 133, 134, 143
Pembroke Dock 65–68
Pioneer Corps 54–55, 57–71, 74, 84, 101,
    106, 108, 161
    87 company 59, 61–67, 84, 101,
    106, 108, 161
Portsmouth 87–88
Protestant Youth Group
    see Bibelkreis
Putsch (1923) 19, 20, 31, 40

Quakers 43, 46
Queen Emma (ship) 98

RAF 113, 115, 119, 134, 151, 163, 164
Raiding Support Regiment (RSR) 124
Ravenna 138, 140, 142
Reichswehr 16, 19, 27, 80
Reimann, Eugene 62
Rome 136–37, 140–41, 159
Royal Engineers 66, 67, 124, 126–28

Royal Marine Commando 11, 70, 88, 91, 109, 118, 144
    No. 40 91
    No. 41 91
Royal Sussex Regiment 74

Salzberger, Rabbi 39
Sarande 120, 124–28
Scotland 75, 91, 165, 166, 168
Shelley, Alfred 135, 136, 142, 171
Sherfield English 160
Sicily 11, 89, 91–110, 143, 169
Sindlingen 147, 151
Snowdonia 74, 85, 86
Spean Bridge 75–80, 168
Speer, Albert 152
Stewart, David (Strauss) 74, 76, 81, 135, 142, 171, 172
Streeten, Paul (Hornig) 91
Syracuse 98

Taranto 111
Tenby (Wales) 65

Tito, Marshal 114, 116, 128, 143
Towyn (Wales) 86
Tripoli 100–01
Tunis 93, 102

Vaughan, Colonel 80
Vegesack 23, 24
Velindre (S. Wales) 64–65
Versailles, Treaty of 17, 31
Villiers, Robbie (Fogel) 74, 81
Vintage Glider Club 167
Vis, island of 11, 112–14, 116, 119, 120

Wales 61–64, 67, 74, 83–86, 168
Wallingford Farm Training Colony 49–52
Wüst, Frau Elsa 39, 43, 151, 153

X-Troops
    see Commandos (3 Troop)

Yugoslav islands 111–17
Yugoslav partisans 114–19, 124, 128, 129